2-
2008

"Better hiring can win you races, and help you win in your career."
—WILLIAM INGRAHAM KOCH, founder and president, the Oxbow Group,
and winner of the 1992 America's Cup sailboat race

"Geoff Smart and Randy Street have done an amazing job distilling the best advice from some of the world's most successful business leaders." — H. WAYNE HUIZENGA, chairman, Huizenga
Holdings, Inc., previously founder &
CEO of Waste Management, Blockbuster
Video, and AutoNation

"A great read—it really is all about finding, keeping, and motivating the team." —JOHN C. MALONE, chairman, Liberty Media Corporation

"The Blackstone Group gives ghSMART straight A's across the board."
—STEPHEN A. SCHWARZMAN, chairman, CEO,
and co-founder, the Blackstone Group

"ghSMART has helped make talent a competitive advantage at Heinz." —WILLIAM R. JOHNSON, chairman, president,
and CEO, H. J. Heinz Corporation

"The best business book I've read in a very long time."
—ERIC COHEN, managing partner, WHI Capital Partners

"Seventy percent of the game is finding the right people, putting them in the right position, listening to them, and alleviating what gets in their way. *Who* is a practical guide to making sure you get the right people to start with! Excellent advice and guide."
—ROBERT J. GILLETTE, president and CEO, Honeywell Aerospace

"No investment is more important than building our teams, and ghSMART helps us do it right."
—KEN GRIFFIN, founder, president, and CEO, Citadel Investment Group

"The key point in this book is that those of us who run companies should include *who* decisions near the top of the list of strategic priorities." —JOHN VARLEY, group chief executive, Barclays

"In real estate, it's location, location, location. In business, it's management, management, management. *Who* tells us how to identify the right management. ghSMART is brilliant."
                                        —JOHN HOWARD, CEO, BSMB

"We have incorporated ghSMART's <u>A</u> Method as a core element of our leadership development curriculum and talent management process. The marked improvement in key business results speaks for itself."   —JOHN ZILLMER, chairman and CEO,
                                        Allied Waste Industries

"ghSMART gets it! Great businesses don't run by themselves, great people get the job done. ghSMART has a proven approach for finding those A Players!"   —MATT LEVIN, managing director, Bain Capital

"Knowing *what* to do is not the major challenge faced by executives—finding *who* to do it is! Here's great advice for a talent-hungry world."
                                        —MARSHALL GOLDSMITH, *New York Times*
                                        bestselling author of *What Got You Here
                                        Won't Get You There*

"CEOs and middle managers can benefit from this book."
                                        —ALEC GORES, founder and chairman,
                                        the Gores Group

"I have used ghSMART to make better *who* decisions for a decade, with excellent results."   —PAUL LATTANZIO, senior managing director,
                                        BGCP

"ghSMART's <u>A</u> Method for Hiring is one of the key processes we use religiously to build a valuable company."
                                        —MICHAEL J. AHEARN, CEO,
                                        First Solar, Inc.

"ghSMART's method works for hiring investors or CEOs."

—MARK GALLOGLY and JEFF H. ARONSON,
co-founders and managing principals,
Centerbridge Partners, L.P.

"*Who* is the only book you need to read if you are serious about making smart hiring and promotion decisions. It is the most actionable book on middle and upper management hiring that I've read after twenty years in HR." —ED EVANS, EVP and chief personnel officer,
Allied Waste Industries

"We asked ghSMART to train our CEOs on the <u>A</u> Method for Hiring. For those who follow it, this method will turn their #1 problem into their greatest strength."

—MARK STONE, senior managing director, the Gores Group

"I went from sales manager to CEO in under five years, thanks to the concepts in this book."

—GREG ALEXANDER, founder and CEO, Sales Benchmark Index, Inc.

"I wish I had this book thirty years ago at the beginning of my career!"

—JAY JORDAN, chairman and CEO, the Jordan Company

"A terrific (and unusual) combination of practical experience and rigorous research." —STEVEN N. KAPLAN, Neubauer Family
Professor of Entrepreneurship and
Finance, University of Chicago
Graduate School of Business

"Those who have read Jim Collins are familiar with the idea of starting with the right *who*. *Who* provides a step-by-step framework to implement this powerful idea. Having participated in ghSMART's process, I can say that the results were incredibly valuable in helping me see what I needed to do to move from being an 'A' candidate to being an 'A' head of school." —KOLIA O'CONNOR, head of school,
Sewickley Academy

"A must read for all those who want to build excellence in their organizations." —STACY SCHUSTERMAN, chairman and CEO, Samson Investment Company

"An exceptional read, uncovering the voodoo interviews and human capital gobbledy gook to offer a simple and real solution to a high stakes problem—picking the right *who*." —KELVIN THOMPSON, managing partner, Heidrick & Struggles

"This book will save you and your company *time* and *money*. In business, what else is there?" —ROGER MARINO, co-founder, EMC Corporation

"A very practical solution to a problem that many managers find difficult to solve." —GABRIEL ECHAVARRÍA, chairman and director, Corona S.A. Organization

"You'll find yourself nodding yes, saying 'That's right,' and thinking, 'Oh, I've been there,' all the way through this grand slam of a book. Whether you're starting a company or running part of a big one, the level of success you achieve is almost always a result of choosing the right people for the right jobs at the right time. It's all about the *who*!" —AARON KENNEDY, founder and chairman, Noodles & Company

"Entrepreneurs live or die based on *who* they hire. In this new book, the team at ghSMART offers simple, practical, and entertaining advice and tips to turn hiring from a source of pain into a source of competitive advantage." —VERNE HARNISH, founder, Entrepreneurs' Organization (EO) and author of *Mastering the Rockefeller Habits*

Who

Who

THE A METHOD FOR HIRING

Geoff Smart AND Randy Street

ghSMART®

BALLANTINE BOOKS / NEW YORK

Published in the United States by Ballantine Books,
an imprint of The Random House Publishing Group,
a division of Random House, Inc., New York.

BALLANTINE and colophon are registered
trademarks of Random House, Inc.

LIBRARY OF CONGRESS CATALOGING-IN-PUBLICATION DATA

Smart, Geoff.
Who : the A method for hiring / by Geoff Smart and Randy Street.
p. cm.
ISBN 978-0-345-50419-7 (hardcover : alk. paper)
1. Employee selection.   2. Employees—Recruiting.
3. Employment interviewing.   I. Street, Randy.   II. Title.
HF5549.5.S38S593 2008
658.3'11—dc22   2008025883

Printed in the United States of America on acid-free paper

www.ballantinebooks.com
www.ghsmart.com

40 39 38 37 36 35 34 33

Book design by Casey Hampton

This book is dedicated to the clients of ghSMART.
Thank you for giving us the honor and privilege of serving you.

CONTENTS

WHO, NOT WHAT

The most important decisions that businesspeople make
are not what *decisions, but* who *decisions.*

—JIM COLLINS, AUTHOR OF *GOOD TO GREAT*

Who is your number-one problem.

Not *what*.

What refers to the strategies you choose, the products and services you sell, and the processes you use. You can spend your whole career chasing solutions to the million *what* problems plaguing your business. That is what most managers do. Unfortunately, focusing solely on the *what* means you will continue to feel stressed, make less money than you desire, and lack the time to do what you want.

Or you can decide today to focus on the *who*.

Who refers to the people you put in place to make the *what* decisions. Who is running your sales force? Who is assembling your product? Who is occupying the corner office? *Who* is where the magic begins, or where the problems start.

Just ask Nate Thompson, the CEO of Spectra Logic. Thompson's company is now thriving. But in the early years, he was such a captive to the poor performers he hired that he couldn't even go on vacation.

It wasn't that Thompson didn't interview thoroughly. He did. He pored over resumes. He often spent hours with each candidate trying to sense the chemistry. He thought all of the people he brought on board looked terrific. Yet many ended up being fundamentally unsuited for the jobs for which they had been hired. One particularly awful hire embezzled over $90,000 in commissions.

"On the commission sheets," Thompson told us, "the sales VP would take those *1*'s that the accountant wrote in and would turn them into *4*'s! This inflated his commission to four times what it was supposed to be."

The financial pain was great, but Thompson suffered personally even more. Employees he had mishired, and the problems they created, made it impossible for him to get away from the office. When he did, Thompson spent most of his time dealing with crises back at work.

"I love to ski. Back in the early days, I would drive my family up to Vail, Colorado. But once we got there, I might as well have been back at work. I couldn't get on the mountain for the first four hours of every day. I had to be on the phone and deal with e-mails, doing the job of people I had mishired. I remember seeing my wife and kids roll their eyes and go out to ski without me."

Sound familiar? Ultimately, *who* failures infect every aspect of our professional and personal lives.

At ghSMART, we are in the business of helping companies make better *who* decisions. Our mission is to use our expertise in human behavior to help CEOs and investors build valuable companies. Geoff Smart is CEO and founded the firm in 1995. Randy Street is a partner in the firm and heads the ghSMART Executive Learning business unit. Our clients include Global 1000 companies and start-ups, and range from Wall Street bankers to passionate leaders of nonprofits. Our work has taken us from Vancouver to Sydney and from Milan to Taiwan as we've helped these clients make over twelve thousand *who* decisions using the method we will show you in this book. And we've trained another thirty thousand managers how to implement it. We've spent years dealing with these issues every day, yet this book is much more than the sum total of our experiences.

To test our observations and to glean new ones, we engaged Dr. Steven N. Kaplan and his team of finance wizards at the Graduate School of Business at the University of Chicago to conduct the largest-ever statistical study of its kind to help understand what types of candidates are successful performers and which are not. Kaplan and his team spent the better part of two years sifting through data we had gathered on over three hundred CEOs to discover some surprising insights.

Most important, we have talked with and listened to many of the world's most talented leaders as they taught us their secrets to hiring success.

More than twenty business billionaires, most of them self-made, have contributed their insights and experiences to this book, an unprecedented assemblage. These are people who have been on the front lines of some of the most exciting and defining business ventures of our times—people whose hiring decisions have sometimes moved markets.

We also talked with over thirty CEOs of multibillion-dollar companies to get their perspectives, and we interviewed dozens of other successful CEOs, managers, investors, nonprofit heads, and experts on management.

All told, we conducted over thirteen hundred hours of interviews and countless additional hours of analysis for this project. We are unaware of any study that matches ours for depth, breadth, and hands-on experience. Most of our focus was on managers rather than HR departments, since making the right *who* decisions is so fundamental to career success. As Joe Mansueto, founder of Morningstar, put it, "Your success as a manager is simply the result of how good you are at hiring the people around you."

Out of this mountain of research, we have identified four parts of the hiring process where failure typically occurs. It does not matter whether a person is being hired as a call-center worker or the CEO of a $50-billion financial services institution. *Who* mistakes happen when managers:

- Are unclear about what is needed in a job
- Have a weak flow of candidates
- Do not trust their ability to pick out the right candidate from a group of similar-looking candidates
- Lose candidates they really want to join their team

These *who* mistakes are *pricey.* According to studies we've done with our clients, the average hiring mistake costs fifteen times an employee's base salary in hard costs and productivity loss. Think about it: a single hiring blunder on a $100,000 employee can cost a company $1.5 million or more. If your business is making ten such mistakes a year, it's pouring $15 million down the drain annually. Nate Thompson estimates his early years of getting *who* wrong cost Spectra Logic as much as $100 million in value.

These *who* mistakes are *prevalent* as well. Peter Drucker and other management gurus have long estimated that the hiring success rate of managers is a dismal 50 percent. Just think of the lost time and energy that represents, not only for you but all through the organization.

What most managers do not know is that *who* problems are also *preventable.*

The purpose of this book is to give you a solution to your number-one problem—to help you make better *who* decisions.

CEOs, middle managers, and front-line supervisors who have benefited from this solution tell us that it is the simplest, most practical, and most effective way to make great *who* decisions they ever learned. The benefits are huge to you, your company, and even your family. Nate Thompson, for one, finally applied the method and now has a winning team and time for vacation.

Decide to make better *who* decisions, and you will enjoy your career more, make more money, and have more time for the relationships that matter most.

Who

ONE

YOUR #1 PROBLEM

What does a *who* problem look like?

Remember the *I Love Lucy* episode where Lucy and Ethel find work at a candy factory? They're supposed to be wrapping chocolates, but they can't keep up with the pace. So instead of letting the candy pass them by, they start shoving it into their mouths, down their shirts, and anywhere else it will fit. That's when a supervisor looks in and congratulates the new hires on the empty conveyor belt. Then she calls to someone in the next room, "Speed it up!" And with that the chaos *really* ensues.

You could spend countless hours trying to optimize the line, but that wouldn't get to the heart of the matter. The supervisor didn't have a conveyor problem. She had a Lucy problem.

The Lucy problem is a *who* problem, but chances are yours is neither as funny nor so far down the chain of command. As an engineering friend of ours often laments, "Managing is easy, except for the people part!"

In an October 2006 cover story, "The Search for Talent," *The Economist* reported that finding the right people is the single biggest problem in business today.* We doubt that surprised most readers. The fact is, virtually every manager struggles to find and hire the talent necessary to drive his or her business forward.

We've all been there. We've all heard the horror stories of the CEO who sank a multibillion-dollar public company, the district manager who allowed his region to fall behind competition, even the executive assistant who couldn't keep a schedule. Most of us have lived those stories and could add dozens more to the list.

Even we have made bad *who* decisions. A few years back, Geoff and his wife hired a nanny we'll call Tammy to look after their children. Unfortunately, Geoff had what his six-year-old calls a "space-out moment" and neglected to apply the method this book describes when he hired her.

Not many months later, Geoff was on the phone in his home office when he saw his two-year-old running naked down the driveway. He immediately hung up on his client and raced outdoors to stop his daughter before she ran into the

* *The Economist,* October 7–13, 2006.

street. Fortunately, the FedEx truck was not barreling up the driveway at that moment.

Then Geoff went looking for Tammy to find out what had happened. All she could say was, "Well, it's hard to keep track of all of the kids." It is, but as Geoff explained to her, that's exactly what she had been hired to do. Sometimes a *who* problem can mean life or death.

Needless to say, Geoff's next nanny search commenced immediately, involved the method presented in this book, and resulted in a much better hire.

The fact is, all of us let our *who* guard down sometimes. We realize how inflated resumes can be. Yet we accept at face value claims of high accomplishment that we know better than to fully trust. Due diligence, after all, takes time, and time is the one commodity most lacking in busy managers' lives.

George Buckley grew up with adoptive parents in a boardinghouse in a rough part of Sheffield, England, went to a school for physically handicapped children, and worked his way up to becoming the successful CEO of two Fortune 500 companies, including 3M, where he works now. It's the sort of background that breeds a healthy skepticism about resumes.

When we met with Buckley, he got straight to the point: "One of the hardest challenges is to hire people from outside the company. One of the basic failures in the hiring process is this: What is a resume? It is a record of a person's career with all of the accomplishments embellished and all the failures removed."

Jay Jordan, CEO of the Jordan Company, told us how he once hired a candidate who looked great on paper but failed in the role. The executive demanded some feedback from Jordan on the day of his termination. Jordan didn't want to add insult to injury, but finally couldn't stop himself from saying, "Look, I hired your resume. But unfortunately, what I got was you!"

Due diligence is also lacking in what Kelvin Thompson, a top executive recruiter with Heidrick & Struggles, calls "the worst mistake boards make—the 'la-di-da' interview: nice lunch, nice chat. They say this is a CEO, and we cannot really interview them. So you have a board who never really interviews the candidates."

The techniques you will learn in the pages that follow will help everyone—boards, hiring managers at every level, even parents hiring a nanny—find the right *who* for whatever position needs filling. The method will do the due diligence for you. It lets you focus on the individual candidates without losing sight of the goals and values of your organization.

Before our method can work to its optimal level, though, chances are you might have to break some bad hiring habits of your own.

VOODOO HIRING

How is it that executives who are so talented in so many ways have such trouble finding the right people for their teams? Steve Kerr, the legendary management expert who built Crotonville for Jack Welch at GE, and who most recently served as managing director and chief learning officer at Goldman Sachs, has a simple answer: "Otherwise smart people struggle to hire strangers. People unfamiliar with great hiring methods consider the process a mysterious black art."

Our experience and our research say the same. In an age in which every other management process has been studied and codified, we find it amazing that people still view hiring, the process where building an organization begins, as something that resists an orderly approach. Yet managers cling to their favorite methods even when evidence suggests they don't work.

Take a moment to consider how you and your managers approach hiring. If you find yourself time and again wondering how a misfit got on the payroll, then we suspect you are using one of the top ten voodoo hiring methods:

1. *The Art Critic.* When it comes to judging art, going on gut instinct sometimes works just fine. A good art critic can make an accurate appraisal of a painting within minutes. With executive hiring, though, people who think they are naturally equipped to "read" people on the fly are setting themselves up to be fooled big-time. Forgers can pass off fake paintings as real ones to the time-pressed buyer, and people who want a job badly enough can fake an interview if it lasts only a few minutes. Gut instinct is terribly inaccurate when it comes to hiring someone. If you extend an offer based on a good gut feel, you are going to have a stomachache!

2. *The Sponge.* A common approach among busy managers is to let everybody interview a candidate. The

goal of this sponge-like behavior is to soak up information by spending as much time with people as possible. Unfortunately, managers rarely coordinate their efforts, leaving everybody to ask the same, superficial questions. We witnessed one interview process where six interviewers in a row asked a candidate about his skydiving hobby. Collectively, they burned over sixty minutes on a topic that had nothing to do with the job—although the fellow was an accomplished sky diver, as it turned out! The Sponge's ultimate assessment of the person he hires rarely goes deeper than "He's a good guy!"

3. *The Prosecutor.* Many managers act like the prosecutors they see on TV. They aggressively question candidates, attempting to trip them up with trick questions and logic problems. Why are manhole covers round? How did the markets do yesterday? One employer we have heard of asks candidates if they play chess. If they say yes, he matches them up against an employee who happens to be a Russian chess master! In the end, trick questions might land you the most knowledgeable candidate, and maybe even someone who can beat a Russian chess master, but knowledge and ability to do the job are not the same thing.

4. *The Suitor.* Rather than rigorously interviewing a candidate, some managers spend all of their energy selling the applicant on the opportunity. Suitors are more concerned with impressing candidates than assessing their capabilities. They spend all of their time in an inter-

view talking and virtually no time listening. Suitors land their share of candidates, but they take their chances with the candidate actually being a good fit.

5. *The Trickster.* Then there are the interviewers who use gimmicks to test for certain behaviors. They might throw a wad of paper on the floor, for example, to see if a candidate is willing to clean it up, or take him to a party to see how he interacts with other partygoers. Use this method, and you are likely to find yourself in the awkward position of explaining to your friends why you fired that nice guy from the party who helped clean up the mess.

6. *The Animal Lover.* Many managers hold on stubbornly to their favorite pet questions—questions they think will reveal something uniquely important about a candidate. One executive takes this literally, telling us that he judged candidates by their answer to one question: "What type of animal would you be?" The question has a truly voodoo answer key. "I look for people who have a witty answer." Not only do questions like this lack any relevance or scientific basis, but they are utterly useless as predictors of on-the-job performance.

7. *The Chatterbox.* This technique has a lot in common with the "la-di-da" interview. The conversation usually goes something like this: "How about them Yankees! Man, the weather is rough this time of year. You grew up in California? So did I!" Although enjoyable, the method does nothing to help you make a good decision. You're supposed to be picking up a future trusted

colleague, not someone with whom you can bat around baseball stats.

8. *The Psychological and Personality Tester. The Handbook of Industrial/Organizational Psychology* recommends against using these types of tests for executive selection decisions, and with good reason. Asking a candidate a series of bubble-test questions like "Do you tease small animals?" or "Would you rather be at a cocktail party or the library on a Friday night?" is not useful (although both are actual questions on popular psychological tests), and it's certainly not predictive of success on the job. Savvy candidates can easily fake the answers based on the job for which they are vying.

9. *The Aptitude Tester.* Tests can help managers determine whether a person has the right aptitude for a specific role, such as persistence for a business development position, but they should never become the sole determinant in a hiring decision. As we'll see in Chapter 2, aptitude is only part of a much larger equation. Use these tests as screening tools if you like, but do not use them in isolation.

10. *The Fortune-Teller.* Just like a fortune-teller looking in a crystal ball to predict the future, some interviewers like to ask their candidates to look into the future regarding the job at hand by asking hypothetical questions: "What would you do? How would you do it? Could you do it?" Fifty years of academic literature on interview methods makes a strong case against using these types of questions during interviews. For exam-

ple, asking, "If you were going to resolve a conflict with a co-worker, how would you do it?" is sure to get the response, "Well, I would sit my co-worker down, listen to her concerns, and design a win-win solution with her." Maybe. Then again, maybe not. The answer sounds nice, but we question how many people would actually do those things. Remember, it's the walk that counts, not the talk.

At the bottom line, all these voodoo hiring methods share an assumption that it's easy to assess a person. Just find the right gimmicks, pop the right quiz, and trust the scattered chicken bones to point the way, and you're certain to have great hiring outcomes. Beyond that, we're all prone to certain cognitive traps. We want to make quick decisions to get on with things. We like to see people as fundamentally truthful. We wish that it were so, but one of the painful truths of hiring is this: *it is hard to see people for who they really are.*

FINDING A PLAYERS

The good news is that a clear and tested path leads the way out of all this hiring mess. Finding A Players begins with setting the bar higher. Unless you're looking to finish in the bottom half of the standings, you would never assemble a team composed largely of B or C Players. Why, then, use hiring methods that are almost certain to bring second-stringers and backups crowding through the front door?

What is an A Player?

For one thing, he or she is not just a superstar. Think of an A Player as the *right* superstar, a talented person who can do the job you need done, while fitting in with the culture of your company. We define an A Player this way: *a candidate who has at least a 90 percent chance of achieving a set of outcomes that only the top 10 percent of possible candidates could achieve.*

Pay attention to the two mathematical elements of that definition. We're saying that you need to initially stack the odds in your favor by hiring people who have at least a 90 percent chance of succeeding in the role you have defined. Not 50 percent, 90 percent. This will take longer in the short run, but it will save you serious time and money down the road.

Then in the second part of the definition we raise the bar. Who cares if somebody has a 90 percent chance of achieving a set of outcomes that just about anybody could accomplish? You don't want to be good. You want to be great, and A Players have a 90 percent chance of accomplishing what only 10 percent of possible hires could accomplish.

Ken Griffin is living proof of the value of hiring A Players. Griffin is the founder and CEO of Citadel, one of the world's most successful hedge funds, with over $20 billion in managed assets, and trading activity across all of its businesses that tops five hundred million shares a day (nearly 10 percent of total United States equity volume).

Those are huge numbers, but Citadel wasn't always such a powerhouse. In fact, Griffin established his firm in 1990 with just over $4 million in seed money from family, friends, and early investors. In these early years, he invested heavily in the technology backbone that differentiates Citadel from its peers, and that paid big dividends. Citadel's long-term investment performance is among the best in the industry.

Clearly, stock picking has been vital to Citadel's glowing bottom line—it's the key *what* of the business. But Griffin has also invested heavily in the talent that drives the company's success—the *who* behind the *what*—and he has no doubt which has been the bigger contributor. He recently told us that he traces an overwhelming percentage of his success back to the people on his team.

Hiring A Players takes hard work. As we'll see, it's not always for the faint of heart. You have to dig hard, ask tough questions, and be prepared sometimes for disturbing answers.

In the process of screening would-be traders for Citadel, Griffin and other executives used the ghSMART process. In one situation, Griffin was speaking to a candidate who looked great on paper and had a stellar reputation. In the course of the interview, Griffin learned that the candidate had worked with a difficult boss. When asked what he did about it, the candidate responded, "I sent an e-mail to all of my colleagues, pointing out that our boss was incompetent." Wrong answer! But Citadel's rigorous use of the method in this book prevented the company from making a critical mistake. Asking the right questions before you bring on your next employee can have a similar effect for your business.

YOU ARE WHO YOU HIRE

In business, you are who you hire. Hire C Players, and you will always lose to the competition. Hire B Players, and you might do okay, but you will never break out. Hire A Players, and life gets very interesting no matter what you are pursuing.

Steve Schwarzman, chairman, CEO, and co-founder of the Blackstone Group, a private equity firm, said, "Hiring A Players is not everything. But it is one of the most important skills to growing a large private equity firm, or growing the value of a company.

"Two years ago, the founding partner of Texas Pacific Group, David Bonderman, and I were reflecting on what mattered in determining our financial returns. After exhaustively studying our databases of dozens of deals across twenty years, we concluded that the keys to success in private equity are: (1) buying right, (2) having an A management team, and (3) selling right. Everything else is just conversation.

"In our portfolio companies, many of which are multibillion-dollar revenue companies, what matters is having: (1) the right strategy in the right market, (2) an A management team, and (3) financial discipline. The difference between an A and a B CEO produces an order of magnitude difference in the return."

How do you get an A team? That's what we at ghSMART have spent thirteen years learning and all the field work for this book testing and refining. We call the solution the "ghSMART A Method for Hiring," or the "A Method" for short. The A Method defines a simple process for identifying and hiring A Players with a high degree of success. It helps you get the *who* right.

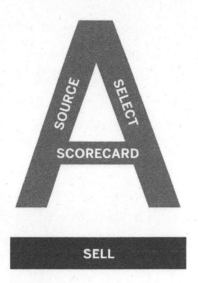

You can think of each line in the letter <u>A</u> and the underline as four steps that build the whole method. The four steps are:

- *Scorecard.* The scorecard is a document that describes exactly what you want a person to accomplish in a role. It is not a job description, but rather a set of outcomes and competencies that define a job done well. By defining A performance for a role, the scorecard gives you a clear picture of what the person you seek needs to be able to accomplish.
- *Source.* Finding great people is getting harder, but it is not impossible. Systematic sourcing *before* you have slots to fill ensures you have high-quality candidates waiting when you need them.
- *Select.* Selecting talent in the <u>A</u> Method involves a series

of structured interviews that allow you to gather the relevant facts about a person so you can rate your scorecard and make an informed hiring decision. These structured interviews break the voodoo hiring spell.

- *Sell.* Once you identify people you want on your team through selection, you need to persuade them to join. Selling the right way ensures you avoid the biggest pitfalls that cause the very people you want the most to take their talents elsewhere. It also protects you from the biggest heartbreak of all—losing the perfect candidate at the eleventh hour.

The simplicity of the <u>A</u> Method means it is easy to understand and implement at all levels, from CEO to receptionist. But the fact that the method is simple doesn't mean that implementing it won't require real effort on your part. The payoff, though, is huge.

One of our clients who put this method to the test was the Blackstone Group. In conjunction with another investor, Apollo, they used the <u>A</u> Method to replace the CEO at an underperforming portfolio company. The company's value had been so flat over five years that some investors referred to it as a "lead balloon." But that was before using the <u>A</u> Method to hire John Zillmer as CEO of Allied Waste.

Board member Tom Hill, vice chairman of Blackstone, played a role in recruiting Zillmer. Hill reflected, "The board agreed we had no choice. We knew that we wanted a CEO who, unlike the previous one, was confident enough to have A

Players around him. John Zillmer was the perfect fit for what we needed."

Over an intense eighteen months, Zillmer hired or promoted twenty-seven new A Players into the management ranks with a 90 percent hiring success rate. Then he worked with his senior vice president of human resources to train every manager in the company on the A Method. Today, Zillmer expects every single manager to build and maintain a team of A Players.

As Zillmer told us, "I think the fastest way to improve a company's performance is to improve the talent of the workforce, whether it is the ultimate leader or someone leading a divisional organization. It just energizes the company and leads to positive things." And doing so energizes the bottom line, too. The value of the company increased 67 percent over the first eighteen months of Zillmer's tenure.

With a little motivation and commitment, you can apply these same principles to your span of control. You might even be in a position to implement them across your entire company, as Zillmer has done.

In these pages, you will find the key to greater financial success and more personal and career satisfaction. The A Method has worked for us. It has worked for hundreds of our clients, organizations of every shape and size. And it will work for you.

TWO

SCORECARD
A Blueprint for Success

Scorecards are your blueprint for success. They take the theoretical definition of an A Player and put it in practical terms for the position you need to fill.

Scorecards describe the mission for the position, outcomes that must be accomplished, and competencies that fit with both the culture of the company and the role. You wouldn't think of having someone build you a house without an architect's blueprint in hand. Don't think of hiring people for your team without this blueprint by your side.

What becomes all too clear in many of our initial meetings with clients is that they don't bother to define what they want before they go hire somebody. We recently worked with a global financial services institution interested in hiring a VP of strategic planning. "What is this role all about?" we asked the executive responsible for the hire.

He replied, "Well, we need someone who can work with the different business units to capture their plans in a master budget. We need an integrated plan, really. The VP of strategic planning can help capture all of the thinking into a single plan."

The executive's manager was also sitting in the room. Just about at this moment, he jumped urgently into the conversation: "That's not what we need at all! We don't need a tactical planner. We need a visionary leader. We need someone who can survey the market and help us devise new strategies and create new products. We need someone to keep us ahead of the competition."

The room buzzed as they debated their conflicting views for the strategic planning role for the next twenty minutes. Finally, the hiring manager said, "I was about to offer my top candidate the job. It sounds like I should put that on hold while we define what we really want."

Bingo!

The first failure point of hiring is not being crystal clear about what you really want the person you hire to accomplish. You may have some vague notion of what you want. Others on your team are likely to have their own equally vague notions of what you want and need. But chances are high that your vague notions do not match theirs. Enter the scorecard, the method we've devised for designing your criteria for a particular position.

Neville Isdell, chairman and former CEO of the Coca-Cola Company, offered an example of this concept at work from his own experience. "In hiring, everything is situational," he told us, "and no situation is entirely replicable. You are going to need different types of leaders at different phases of organizations.

"When I was coming into Coca-Cola as CEO, I needed to bring in a new head of human resources. We had been through significant issues with morale, and the HR function was probably ranked at the bottom in terms of respect and regard from the employees as a whole. I needed somebody who could bring about change by building coalitions, but who could still do it with energy, drive, and speed. That meant I needed somebody with high emotional intelligence, really strong knowledge of the business, really good interpersonal skills, and the ability to build bridges. That was one type of situation that required one type of person." Having this kind of clarity about the situational need enabled Isdell to put Cynthia McCague in the position, who has succeeded for exactly the reasons Isdell had anticipated.

The scorecard is composed of three parts: the job's mission, outcomes, and competencies. Together, these three pieces describe A performance in the role—what a person must accomplish, and how. They provide a clear linkage between the people you hire and your strategy.

MISSION: THE ESSENCE OF THE JOB

The mission is an executive summary of the job's core purpose. It boils the job down to its essence so everybody understands why you need to hire someone into the slot. Take a look at the sample scorecard on the next page. The mission for the VP of sales clearly captures why the role exists: to grow revenue through direct contacts with industrial customers. That's it. It isn't to build channel sales. It isn't to seek new industry verticals. It isn't to serve as an administrator.

For a mission to be meaningful, it has to be written in plain language, not the gobbledygook so commonly found in business today. Here is a perfect example of what *not* to do: "The mission for this role is to maximize shareholder value by leveraging core assets of the NPC division while minimizing communication deficiencies and obfuscations."

That's an exaggeration, but not by much. We bet you could find nonsensical statements like this floating around your company. And we bet further that whoever wrote them didn't have a clue what the job really was or needed to be. Removing the clutter keeps your missions short, sweet, and, most of all, understandable.

You'll know you have a good mission when candidates, recruiters, and even others from your team understand what you are looking for without having to ask clarifying questions. In the case of the financial services company we cited earlier, the disconnect surrounding the strategic planning role never would have existed with a clearly articulated mission. It could

Sample Scorecard

Mission for VP Sales
CleanMax USA, Inc.

To double our revenue over three years by signing large profitable contracts with industrial customers. And to set up one hunting team to land new accounts and one farming team to grow existing accounts.

Outcomes	Rating & Comments

1. Grow revenue from $25 million to $50 million by end of year three (25% annual growth).
- Increase number of national industrial customers from four in year one to eight in year two to ten in year three.
- Reduce revenue from residential customers from 75% of total sales by end of year three.

2. Increase EBITDA margin from 9% to 15% by end of year three.
- Increase fluffo-matic 70% margin add-on sales from 33% to 90% of all customer orders by end of year one.

3. Topgrade the sales organization by end of year one.
- Hire an A player Director of Outside Sales by end of year one.
- Hire an A player Director of Inside Sales by end of year one.
- Fire any sales rep who has not made quota by end of year one.

4. Deliver monthly forecast reports that are 90% accurate.

5. Design and roll out sales training to all client-facing employees by end of year two.

have been something along the lines of this: "To serve as a visionary leader who helps the bank capture market share from the competition by analyzing the market and devising successful new strategies and product offerings." That's a mission anyone in the business can understand.

Don't Hire the Generalist. Hire the Specialist.

Mission statements help you avoid one of the most common hiring traps: hiring the all-around athlete. All-around athletes are the candidates who walk into our offices bearing impressive pedigrees, polished attire, and admirable accomplishments in a wide variety of roles. They seem to be able to do it all. They speak well, learn quickly, offer broad insights on company strategy, and convince us that they can adapt to virtually any challenge or task the company might place on their shoulders.

In theory, who wouldn't want someone like that on the team? Yet one of the most consistent findings from our interviews with dozens upon dozens of CEOs and top executives is that hiring all-around athletes rarely works. By definition, they are generalists. That's their charm. They are good at many things and can wear lots of different hats. But job requirements are rarely general. If you've defined the position correctly from the outset, you should be looking for narrow but deep competence.

Think of it in medical terms. A family-practice doctor is great so long as you're seeing him for the usual run of coughs, colds, and cholesterol tests. But when the diagnosis is tough to make or the problem is life-threatening, you're going to go to a specialist as quickly as you can. You wouldn't let your family-practice doctor perform open-heart surgery on you, and in the same way you shouldn't look for a full team of generalists to solve your business problems. The mission should help you find not the generalist who points you to the problem but the very best specialist to help you solve it.

As Nick Chabraja, the CEO of General Dynamics, puts it, "I think success comes from having the right person in the right job at the right time with the right skill set *for the business problem that exists.*"

He went on to explain: "I've screwed up that one. We have not done this right every time. There is a tendency to gravitate to the best all-around athlete; you know—tremendous skill set, resume that is knock-your-socks-off.

"Early in my tenure I made that choice with a very capable executive. He was innovative, creative, and a splendid business developer. He could conceive of programs and sell them to the customer. But that was not my problem. We had a huge backlog and I needed a guy who could run operations. It was a matter of mining the backlog. So I made the mistake of putting in place a guy who went on to put *more* orders in the backlog. Operating margins actually went down. It took me a couple of years to address the mistake.

"The moral of the story was that I later got a guy whose skill set exactly matched the job at hand. He did gangbusters for us. He was all operations. He was probably the best at it in the world. The other guy went on elsewhere to a splendid career where his role matched his skill set."

We heard much the same from Alec Gores, the founder and chairman of the Gores Group, a private equity firm based in Los Angeles. Over the past twenty years, Gores' deals have created over $1 billion in value while losing only $2 million in the process, a truly astonishing record. Like Nick Chabraja, Gores has learned to rely on people with job-specific talents, rather than gunning for all-around athletes.

"Each target and company has different needs for the CEO and any management role," he says. "I look at our team almost like a football team. If I am hiring for a position, I ask myself, what is this person going to be doing? Are they a quarterback? A center? I don't try to get the quarterback to operate like a center or a linebacker."

A final caution about mission. You can't just pull a mission off the shelf and dust it off whenever the position needs refilling. Every environmental interest group in Washington, D.C., needs congressional liaisons—that's part of the core business—but issues change, new expertise is required, political power and committee chairs shift on Capitol Hill. The more a new liaison can plug into all those constituencies and the more mastery he or she has of the subject, the better the chances of being heard. That's why scorecards need to be evolving documents, not static ones.

Arthur Rock, one of the most successful private equity investors in history and an early investor into Intel, put this into sharp perspective for us when he shared his insights on Intel's early years. "It was all about having the right people in the right spots at the right time in the case of Intel. Bob Noyce was the inventor and promoter, then Gordon Moore was the technologist, and then Andy Grove was the driver."

Not only did Rock evaluate Intel's needs at each point in its history; he deliberately sought leaders whose skills were optimized for each phase of the company's growth. While each CEO was generally talented, all three brought something different to the table along the way. The results speak for themselves. Intel's succession of "specialists" drove the company's market capitalization to well over $100 billion and led it to the dominant position in the global semiconductor industry. We would hope the same for your business.

OUTCOMES: DEFINING WHAT MUST GET DONE

Outcomes, the second part of a scorecard, describe what a person needs to accomplish in a role. Most of the jobs for which we hire have three to eight outcomes, ranked by order of importance.

Take another look at the sample scorecard on page 23. Notice how the first outcome in the scorecard reads, "Grow revenue from $25 million to $50 million by end of year three." Either a sales vice president can close $50 million of business by the end of year three or he can't. An A Player will be able to, and a B or C Player won't. Outcomes are that clear, and because they are, they cull the pool of possible candidates right from the start.

People don't want to fail, and they don't want to go through the dislocation of moving to another company, or possibly another city or country, if they know their chances of success are minimal. Set the outcomes high enough—but still within reason—and you'll scare off B and C Players even as you pull in the kind of A Players who thrive on big challenges that fit their skills.

While typical job descriptions break down because they focus on activities, or a list of things a person *will be doing* (calling on customers, selling), scorecards succeed because they focus on outcomes, or what a person *must get done* (grow revenue from $25 million to $50 million by the end of year three). Do you see the distinction?

Sales jobs provide particularly crisp outcomes because assigning numerical targets for sales roles is very straightforward. You sell it or you don't.

Not all jobs allow you to quantify the outcome so easily. In these cases, seek to make the outcomes as objective and observable as possible. For example, an outcome for a marketing manager might read, "Create and implement a new marketing campaign within 180 days of start date." For a community outreach coordinator, you could specify increased visibility or greater and more varied attendance at community forums. You can easily observe whether your new marketing person creates the campaign on time, and you can count heads at community gatherings. Measuring the success of a marketing or visibility campaign is obviously harder, but our clients over the years have come up with plenty of objective criteria, everything from customer feedback to plans delivered on time to budgets met.

Ironically, all that specificity frees new hires to give the job their best shot. They know what they'll be judged on. They know what the company and the boss think is important in their position. Instead of guessing how to do well and careening among a dozen different fronts, they have the game plan right in front of them. That's liberating, not confining.

COMPETENCIES: ENSURING BEHAVIORAL FIT

Competencies flow directly from the first two elements of the scorecard. The mission defines the essence of the job to a high degree of specificity. Outcomes describe what must be accomplished. Competencies define *how* you expect a new hire to operate in the fulfillment of the job and the achievement of the outcomes.

What competencies really count?

For a broad answer to that question, we asked our colleagues at the University of Chicago to analyze our database to determine what competencies ultimately mattered for CEO success. We also asked the many CEOs and other leaders we interviewed for this book to tell us what competencies they felt were most important for the people they have hired. Then we merged the two and prioritized the findings. Those results are shown here:

Critical Competencies for A Players

- *Efficiency.* Able to produce significant output with minimal wasted effort.
- *Honesty/integrity.* Does not cut corners ethically. Earns

trust and maintains confidences. Does what is right, not just what is politically expedient. Speaks plainly and truthfully.

- *Organization and planning.* Plans, organizes, schedules, and budgets in an efficient, productive manner. Focuses on key priorities.
- *Aggressiveness.* Moves quickly and takes a forceful stand without being overly abrasive.
- *Follow-through on commitments.* Lives up to verbal and written agreements, regardless of personal cost.
- *Intelligence.* Learns quickly. Demonstrates ability to quickly and proficiently understand and absorb new information.
- *Analytical skills.* Able to structure and process qualitative or quantitative data and draw insightful conclusions from it. Exhibits a probing mind and achieves penetrating insights.
- *Attention to detail.* Does not let important details slip through the cracks or derail a project.
- *Persistence.* Demonstrates tenacity and willingness to go the distance to get something done.
- *Proactivity.* Acts without being told what to do. Brings new ideas to the company.

Over the years, we've developed a list of competencies that we hand out when we are introducing new clients to the <u>A</u> Method for Hiring. The list begins with the competencies we just shared. In addition, you might want to consider some of the following competencies. These are in unprioritized order:

- *Ability to hire A Players (for managers)*. Sources, selects, and sells A Players to join a company.
- *Ability to develop people (for managers)*. Coaches people in their current roles to improve performance, and prepares them for future roles.
- *Flexibility/adaptability*. Adjusts quickly to changing priorities and conditions. Copes effectively with complexity and change.
- *Calm under pressure*. Maintains stable performance when under heavy pressure or stress.
- *Strategic thinking/visioning*. Able to see and communicate the big picture in an inspiring way. Determines opportunities and threats through comprehensive analysis of current and future trends.
- *Creativity/innovation*. Generates new and innovative approaches to problems.
- *Enthusiasm*. Exhibits passion and excitement over work. Has a can-do attitude.
- *Work ethic*. Possesses a strong willingness to work hard and sometimes long hours to get the job done. Has a track record of working hard.
- *High standards*. Expects personal performance and team performance to be nothing short of the best.
- *Listening skills*. Lets others speak and seeks to understand their viewpoints.
- *Openness to criticism and ideas*. Often solicits feedback and reacts calmly to criticism or negative feedback.
- *Communication*. Speaks and writes clearly and articulately without being overly verbose or talkative. Main-

tains this standard in all forms of written communication, including e-mail.

- *Teamwork*. Reaches out to peers and cooperates with supervisors to establish an overall collaborative working relationship.
- *Persuasion*. Able to convince others to pursue a course of action.

Both lists highlight competencies to consider as you build a scorecard, but they are starter suggestions only. Because every job has different requirements and every scorecard different outcomes, every set of competencies needs to be tailored to the position in question and the peculiar nature of the hiring institution. In practice, people can achieve the same outcome using two different approaches, so we recommend that you do not create too narrow a competency list. For example, two non-profit leaders might approach fund-raising differently. One might rely on his creativity and direct marketing skills to raise funds by sending colorful brochures to a large number of potential donors. Another high performer might rely on direct sales skills and persistence to call on donors directly. There is more than one way to skin a cat.

We use the competencies section of our scorecards as a checklist during the interview process, but we encourage clients to personalize it to fit their individual needs. Many, we've found, have already done that, formally or informally. Bill Johnson, the CEO of Heinz since 1998, is one of them.

"*Chemistry* is always important for both the individual and the company," Johnson said. "If I don't have good chemistry with you, and you don't have good chemistry with me, then skip it. Connecting with them personally is important. That becomes obvious in my initial conversations with a candidate.

"Number two is *commitment*. Theirs to you and yours to them. That is a difficult thing to assess, but it really matters. I want people who are committed.

"Third, are they *coachable*? I underestimated this earlier in my career. You can pass on learning and shortcut their development if they are.

"Number four is, do they have their *ego under control*? Are they prepared to address the problem? If they are thinking about the next job, they will fail. They must be focused on the job they have.

"Number five, do they have the *requisite intellect*?"

Johnson's list has elements in common with the master list of competencies highlighted in our research findings with our University of Chicago colleagues. Like our industry leaders, he values intellect, for example, but not at the expense of other qualities. We have all known smart workers who have been rendered effectively ineffective by a raging ego or an inability to listen. The larger point, though, is that Bill Johnson's list captures what he values most for people who report to him, regardless of role. Make sure yours does the same.

CULTURAL COMPETENCIES: ENSURING ORGANIZATIONAL FIT

Competencies work at two levels. They define the skills and behaviors required for a job, and they reflect the broader demands of your organizational culture. Job competencies are generally easier to list, but cultural fit is just as important.

In our interviews for this book, fully one in three of the billionaires and CEOs we talked with told us that not evaluating cultural fit was one of the biggest reasons for hiring mistakes. People who don't fit fail on the job, even when they are perfectly talented in all other respects.

Evaluating cultural fit obviously begins with evaluating your company's culture. That takes time and energy but often yields insights whose usefulness goes beyond the hiring process.

Try gathering your leadership team in a room and asking this simple question: "What adjectives would you use to describe our culture?" Jot down their responses on a flip chart or whiteboard. It won't take long before a picture emerges. We recently put a new client through this exercise. Soon the room buzzed with words such as *analytical, fast-paced,* and *informal.* It may have been quick and dirty, but it was honest, and that honesty meant they could focus their hiring in the short term on people who could handle all of that. In the longer term, they can still think hard about where the company needs to be heading culturally and become proactive about setting the course in that direction.

Evaluating culture sometimes means removing people who are not a fit. The best salesperson in the world is the wrong hire if you value respect for others and he is openly disrespectful. Who cares how well he can sell if he is going to demoralize the rest of your team? We saw a client fire her single most productive salesperson because he was so argumentative. The team worked far more effectively without his negative influence, and quickly covered the revenue gap left by his departure.

Culture fits—or misfits—inevitably affect the bottom line, but they are about much more than money. George Hamilton, the president of the not-for-profit Institute for Sustainable Communities, told us a story any Fortune 500 CEO could sympathize with.

"We wanted a real star for this position that was coming open in one of our countries. So we recruited this very bright, passionate, and unusual guy, and he did an amazing job. On his own, basically, he turned around the president and parliament on AIDS. They had taken the position that AIDS resulted from immorality. He not only got them to apply successfully for a big global AIDS grant; he also convinced them to set up a strong prevention program.

"But he was an unbelievable pain to work with. Our culture is collaborative, not competitive, but he was one of those people who is so far ahead of everyone intellectually that he couldn't suffer any fools—and that amounted to about 99 percent of us at ISC as far as he was concerned.

"We had this emotional meeting where I praised his work but told him he had to bring other people along. His answer was, 'Look, George, I know I'm high-maintenance.' Then he went on to give both a brilliant and extremely accurate critique of himself from my perspective and a further critique of our lack of field support for him that was so accurate we used it as a work plan to improve our delivery.

"In the end, though, it just wasn't workable. His approach

was so counterproductive that everyone began dissing every-thing he wanted. I had to ask him to leave."

Aaron Kennedy, the chairman and entrepreneur founder of Noodles & Company, a casual restaurant chain with 225 stores around North America, recounted a similar story of how a cultural mismatch undermined his first CEO and imper-iled the company itself.

"I hired a CEO from a big company a few years ago. Our values include respect for our own employees and an emphasis on quality and customer service. We are also a fast-moving, aggressive culture with clear communication and expectations. I didn't fully appreciate how many aspects of our philosophy we would need to have alignment on for this 'CEO transplant' to work."

Kennedy's CEO ended up frustrating the team and seri-ously jeopardized the financial performance of the company.

"Over time, it became clear to the board that important things weren't getting accomplished and the things that were, weren't being done very well. We wondered why. Well, one day directly after a leadership team meeting, I bumped into our VP of operations and he said, 'There went four hours of my life that I'll never get back again.'

"I asked him what he meant, and he simply said, 'We just spent four hours in a leadership team meeting and no deci-sions were made or communicated. We all left unclear about where we're going, who is supposed to do what, or what's the time frame for a decision. Nothing was resolved.' Of course, this was a blazing red light for an action-oriented entrepre-neur like me.

"The energy level, morale, and financial performance of the company had fallen far enough that one of our early leaders and a longtime friend of mine was willing to identify the elephant in the room. He came into my office, closed the door, and said, 'Things have gotten pretty bad. You should ask a few of the other members of the leadership team how they are doing. I think you'll hear that they are very frustrated and are contemplating their alternatives to this job.'

"I learned from each of them that they were deeply disturbed about the course of the company and had grown to dread coming to work. They expressed to me that Noodles & Company had gone from being their favorite thing about life to a cancer that was eating away a little bit of them every day."

With that, Kennedy swiftly removed the culturally mismatched CEO, who admitted that the role was not working for him, either.

"Perhaps it was my fault," Kennedy reflected for us. "Perhaps it was his. But my feeling is that the chemistry just wasn't there. It was a very poor match from the start. Like a heart donor and recipient, there has to be a match or the body of the recipient will reject the new organ. That's exactly what happened."

Kennedy hired another CEO. This time he purposely paid more attention to cultural success factors in choosing his successor. The new CEO, Kevin Reddy, has turned out to be "exactly what we needed," said Kennedy. "He has all of the right values we need. And he has a level of professionalism that really took us to the next level as a company."

What kind of culture do you want to build? Maybe you're

like two of our clients who hire an unusually high number of Ph.D.'s to help them innovate. If so, you should include intelligence on your competency list for every job. Or maybe, like Aaron Kennedy, you've learned the hard way that you value open communication and decisiveness. If so, include those on your competency list for every job, not just for the CEO and senior team.

Don't be afraid to write down what might seem blindingly evident. In the heat of a hiring crisis, the clearest things sometimes get overlooked. By translating your culture and values into a series of competencies that matter for every job, you can avoid making the mistake of not evaluating candidates for the cultural fits that are absolutely crucial to your enterprise.

When Mark Gallogly and Jeff Aronson co-founded Centerbridge Partners in 2007, they raised the largest first-time buyout fund in history, $3.2 billion. Even more impressive, more than 90 percent of the people they hired to manage this massive fund proved to be A Players, despite pulling the team together from scratch during their first year in business. How did they do it? Centerbridge Partners developed a very specific set of hiring criteria that fit its business strategy and culture.

"It is not by chance that we achieved more than 90 percent hiring success," Gallogly now says. "We were clear about what types of people we were looking for."

The Centerbridge scorecard specified that each investment professional had to be able to build trust and gain respect from the management teams they invested in, rather than bullying them, traits not necessarily guaranteed in this hard-driving line of work. They didn't beat around the bush, either. Key competencies for every role included specifically "treats people with respect" and "trustworthiness."

This scorecard approach was put to the test when they discovered that an otherwise highly impressive candidate was known for being disrespectful and harsh with colleagues and management teams. The candidate performed well, but he had been reprimanded in a previous job for "saying the *f*-word numerous times" during a negotiation with the opposing side's lawyers.

That was all Jeff Aronson needed to hear. "Part of successful hiring means having the discipline to pass on talented people who are not a fit," he told us. "One of the toughest decisions we made in our first year was not hiring this talented investor because his challenging personality could have damaged our firm."

Scorecards are the guardians of your culture. They encapsulate on paper the unwritten dynamics that make your company what it is, and they ensure you think about those things with every hiring decision. That's time very well spent.

FROM SCORECARD TO STRATEGY

The beauty of scorecards is that they are not just documents used in hiring. They become the blueprint that links the theory of strategy to the reality of execution. Scorecards translate your business plans into role-by-role outcomes and create alignment among your team, and they unify your culture and ensure people understand your expectations. No wonder they are such powerful management tools.

Scorecards begin with your strategy. You probably have an annual planning cycle of some sort that culminates in a business plan for the coming year. Ever since Peter Drucker coined the term "management by objectives" a half century ago, companies have been paying homage to the need to translate annual business plans into objectives and budgets, but organizations are rarely so good at assigning outcomes for achieving objectives *to the individuals* on the team.

At a keynote speech at a *Fortune* magazine conference a couple of years ago, we asked the two hundred CEOs in the room, "How many of you have in place written objectives for all of your direct reports?" Only 10 percent raised their hands. One in ten! How are people supposed to know what to focus on or how hard to push if you don't identify their objectives? How can you know if your people are performing as well as they should? It's astonishing how few managers use written objectives.

Scorecards solve that problem and ensure not just that you have A Players but that the A Players are delivering A performances.

A good scorecard process translates the objectives of the strategy into clear outcomes for the CEO and senior leadership team. The senior team then translates their outcomes to the scorecards of those below them, and so on. Everybody in the organization ends up with a set of outcomes that support the strategy, and competencies that support the outcomes and culture.

EMC, the data storage company, recognized that it could beat its competitors by focusing on great service instead of just selling data-storage boxes, and the company made service central to its strategy. Entrepreneur and self-made billionaire Roger Marino, the M in EMC, executed this strategy by holding everybody EMC hired and employed, from top to bottom, accountable for great service.

"The thing we valued at EMC was the willingness to go one more step than the next guy, to go one more step to service the customer," Marino told us. "Sometimes people feel that they have such a good widget that they leave the customer by the wayside. That has become prevalent in all industries, not just high-tech. One reason we did so well at EMC was that we serviced our customers a lot better than the competitors. To accomplish that, we specifically hired people who had an unusually high customer service attitude."

Marino wasn't hiring merely to fill a position. He was hiring to reinforce corporate strategy and culture, and he held the people he brought in accountable for accomplishing and demonstrating that every day. The results speak for themselves.

Properly constructed and used, scorecards spread strategy through every aspect of your organizational life. Scorecards:

- Set expectations with new hires
- Monitor employee progress over time
- Objectify your annual review system
- Allow you to rate your team annually as part of a talent review process

Doug Williams, for one, has discovered the power of the scorecard in his business. He is the founder and CEO of iHealth Technologies, a company owned by Goldman Sachs that uses our hiring method.

As Williams told us, "If we spend seven to eight hours interviewing candidates and get the right one, it's an easy return on our investment. The crux comes down to active scorecard management—that is, linking our business plan to people's jobs. The whole key, whether you are hiring, promoting, or managing for performance in the current job, is that you have clear expectations. Having a clear, focused approach helps us be better managers and therefore helps the people we hire have a higher likelihood of success."

Sure, we all want our employees to be great at everything, but in fact few are, and those who are may well demand higher salaries that make us pay for "features" that we don't need. Remember, it's all about the specific skill set you need, when you need it.

"A scorecard forces the manager to make choices and be consistent with those choices," Williams continued. "Scorecard management is hard, but it has great payback. Our hiring success rate has significantly improved, as well as slotting people into assignments that align well with their skills and gifts. The result of both is successful employees and a successful company."

THE SCORECARD IN ACTION: A CASE HISTORY

Sewickley Academy, an independent prekindergarten to grade twelve school on the outskirts of Pittsburgh, engaged ghSMART to help them select a new Head of School.

The board decided that the mission for the role was to improve the curriculum for the students, strengthen the faculty and staff, and put the school on even stronger financial footing.

Three of their top outcomes, not surprisingly, were to (1) by the end of the first year, improve the scope and sequence of the curriculum such that students had a seamless experience, (2) build a team of 90 percent or more A Player teachers and division heads within the first year, and (3) increase fundraising to a specific target while reversing the budget deficit. Other scorecard outcomes addressed technology, diversity, crisis management, and athletics.

The board decided on a few competencies that really mattered to fit the culture they wanted to build and support the outcomes for the role. They wanted someone who was professional, disciplined, caring, fair, and diplomatic. They also wanted someone who would set high standards and hold people accountable for meeting them.

The board found three candidates and was initially attracted to two who had recent classroom backgrounds. One was a particularly warm and outgoing teacher, the other a very smart Ph.D. They initially disregarded their third candidate, Kolia O'Connor, because he came across as too "corporate" and aggressive.

Yet by comparing each of these three people's track records to the scorecard, we found that O'Connor was actually the best fit. He had started out as a teacher and later became a very effective administrator who built strong faculty and staff. He was aggressive and disciplined, but also caring. In fact, the se-

HOW TO CREATE A SCORECARD

1. **MISSION.** Develop a short statement of one to five sentences that describes why a role exists. For example, "The mission for the customer service representative is to help customers resolve their questions and complaints with the highest level of courtesy possible."

2. **OUTCOMES.** Develop three to eight specific, objective outcomes that a person must accomplish to achieve an A performance. For example, "Improve customer satisfaction on a ten-point scale from 7.1 to 9.0 by December 31."

3. **COMPETENCIES.** Identify as many role-based competencies as you think appropriate to describe the behaviors someone must demonstrate to achieve the outcomes. Next, identify five to eight competencies that describe your culture and place those on every scorecard. For example, "Competencies include efficiency, honesty, high standards, and a customer service mentality."

4. **ENSURE ALIGNMENT AND COMMUNICATE.** Pressure-test your scorecard by comparing it with the business plan and scorecards of the people who will interface with the role. Ensure that there is consistency and alignment. Then share the scorecard with relevant parties, including peers and recruiters.

niors at one of his previous schools had dedicated their yearbook to him based on how he handled the deaths of several of their parents. The other two candidates were brainy, but neither demonstrated a track record of getting things done.

The data we gathered in the hiring process proved to the board that O'Connor was a strong fit for the scorecard, and they hired him for this challenging head-of-school post. Five

years later, he has successfully reversed a budget deficit, reduced tuition increases, increased annual giving to record levels, hired nine A Player faculty members, overhauled the
curriculum, and even instituted Mandarin Chinese classes.

As the chairman of the selection committee told us, "We
found the process of gathering data from each candidate and
comparing it to our scorecard very helpful and worthwhile. It
really enriched our process."

With a blueprint for success in hand, you are now ready for
the second step in the <u>A</u> Method, finding the people who can
deliver the A performance specified by your scorecard.

THREE

SOURCE
Generating a Flow of A Players

Getting great candidates does not happen without significant effort. The CEOs of billion-dollar companies that we interviewed for this book recognize recruitment as one of their most important jobs. They consider themselves chief recruiting officers and expect all of their managers to view their jobs the same way.

These successful executives don't allow recruiting to become a one-time event, or something they have to do only every now and then. They are always sourcing, always on the lookout for new talent, always identifying the *who* before a new hire is really needed.

The traditional hiring process looks something like this. A

vacancy opens up in a manager's division, and the manager panics. He has no idea how he is going to fill the spot, so he calls HR and begs for help. HR asks him for a job description, which he copies from an old one he finds and submits to the HR team to post.

Predictably, three months go by without much traction until, getting desperate, the manager pushes the HR team to source more people. Finally, HR presents a few candidates to the manager, and since nobody in the firm knows anything about these people, they subject the candidates to multiple forms of voodoo hiring methods with the hope of making a good decision. Months later, the manager fills the position with one of these unknowns.

Take a moment and think about how passive such an approach is. It relies on finding people in "talent pools" at particular points of need. Yet we all know that talent pools grow stagnant. Like tidal pools far from the ocean's edge, talent pools rarely contain the most vital and energetic candidates. In fact, these traditional talent sources are so overworked that most of the people left in them are not the ones you would want to hire.

Little wonder that the most frequent question we receive in workshops is "How do I source A Players?" Clearly managers at all levels are frustrated by what they perceive as the lack of innovation on this topic.

We observe that many managers source candidates by placing advertisements in one form or another. The overwhelming evidence from our field interviews is that ads are a good way to generate a tidal wave of resumes, but a lousy way to gener-

ate the right flow of candidates. Other methods include using recruiters and recruiting researchers, although success depends heavily on the quality of the actual recruiter assigned to your search.

Of all the ways to source candidates, the number one method is to ask for referrals from your personal and professional networks. This approach may feel scary and timecon-suming, but it is the single most effective way to find potential A Players.

This is an instance where innovation matters far less than process and discipline.

REFERRALS FROM YOUR PROFESSIONAL AND PERSONAL NETWORKS

The industry leaders we interviewed didn't speak with one voice on every topic, but on the subject of sourcing new talent through referrals they were nearly unanimous. Without any prompting from us, a full 77 percent of them cited referrals as

Top-Five Best Methods for Sourcing Talent

Source	How Often Mentioned
1. Referrals from business network.	77%
2. Referrals from personal network.	77%
3. Hire external recruiter.	65%
4. Hire a recruiting researcher.*	47%
5. Hire internal recruiter.	24%

* A recruiting researcher is responsible for using the Internet and phone to generate a list of possible candidates, but is not typically responsible for conducting interviews.

their top technique for generating a flow of the right candidates for their businesses. Yet among average managers it is the least often practiced approach to sourcing.

Take Patrick Ryan, who grew Aon Corporation from a start-up in 1964 to a $13 billion company. "I am not really smarter than the next guy," he told us. "There are lots of smart people in business. I guess the one thing that I have done over the years that is different from most people is that I am constantly on the hunt for talented people to bring into my company.

"I set a goal of personally recruiting thirty people a year to Aon. And I ask my managers to do the same. We are constantly asking people we know to introduce us to the talented people they know."

Ryan's approach is among the easiest we have seen. Whenever he meets somebody new, he asks this simple, powerful question: "Who are the most talented people you know that I should hire?" Talented people know talented people, and they're almost always glad to pass along one another's names. Ryan captures those names on a list, and he makes a point of calling a few new people from his list every week. Then he stays in touch with those who seem to have the most promise.

You can almost certainly identify ten extremely talented people off the top of your head. Calling your list of ten and asking Patrick Ryan's simple question—"Who are the most talented people you know that I should hire?"—can easily generate another fifty to one hundred names. Keep doing this, and in no time you will have moved into many other networks and enriched your personal talent pool with real ability.

But don't stop there. Bring your broader business contacts in on the hunt, too. Ask your customers for the names of the most talented salespeople who call on them. Ask your business partners who they think are the most effective business developers. Do the same with your suppliers to identify their strongest purchasing agents. Join professional organizations and ask the people you meet through events. People you interact with every day are the most powerful sources of talent you will ever find.

The concept extends into your personal and social networks. We suspect that one of the first questions you get asked when you meet someone new is "What do you do?" Next time you answer that question (probably in the next week or two if our experience is any guide), follow up with "Say, now that I have told you what I do, who are the most talented people you know who could be a good fit for my company?" Do that, and you will turn a common social question into a sourcing opportunity.

After years of asking for referrals and personally recruiting people into his company, Patrick Ryan has become a master talent spotter. Not only has he personally sourced many of the executives who lead Aon today, but he spotted and landed his ultimate successor as well.

"I've always believed that senior hiring should be targeted hiring," he said. "I thought it was time for us to find my successor. It is not something to really put off. You should take a lot of time in doing that."

Ryan let the board search committee do its job, but he also offered names from his own network, including Gregory Case, whom Ryan had first met when Case was at McKinsey, the strategy consulting firm.

"He was only forty-two at the time. He had run a big division of McKinsey. People would say he did not have CEO experience, corporate experience, or public corporate experience. I thought he could overcome those because not only was he smart and hardworking, but also he was going to lead, have vision, and take the group along with him. What's more, Greg brought talented people with him."

All this didn't happen overnight. As he did with others in the talent pool he had built through referrals, Ryan nurtured his relationship with Case over a period of many years before finally convincing Case to succeed him as CEO.

Ryan did the same thing when he hired his new general

counsel, Cameron Findlay, whom he had met when Findlay was a lawyer at Sidley Austin, one of the largest law firms in the United States.

"He was number one in his Harvard Law School class. He had a great academic background and had a very successful background as a lawyer. I maintained a relationship with him while he was in the George W. Bush administration. I figured it was time to see him since that administration's first term was winding down. I told him I really wanted him to join Aon. I was the first person to call Cam, and he joined us."

What sets Patrick Ryan apart from so many other executives is how he actively built his network through referrals, then followed up with high-potential candidates to maintain the relationship. He kept his sourcing network alive and constantly renewed. And because he was disciplined about doing so, he didn't have to go looking when a position opened up at Aon, including his own job. Ryan was already right in the midst of a flow of great candidates.

REFERRALS FROM EMPLOYEES

As valuable as outside referrals are, in-house ones often provide better-targeted sourcing. After all, who knows your needs and culture better than the people who are already working for you? Yet while this is far from a blinding insight, we're constantly amazed at how few managers actually take the time to ask their employees for help.

Selim Bassoul, the chairman and CEO of Middleby Corporation, told us that employee referrals have been an incredible source of A Players as he doubled his business over the last five years.

"Our employees became our number-one recruiting technique," he said. "We told the employees, 'If you spot somebody like us, at a customer, at a supplier, or at a competitor, we want to hire them.' That became very successful. People would say there is a great person there; let's go after them. Employees referred 85 percent of our new hires!"

Paul Tudor Jones, president and founder of Tudor Investment Corporation, also leverages referrals from his existing employees. "It takes A Players to know A Players," he reasons with good cause. "Our success rate is 60 percent higher for people who are referred by somebody else in our firm."

At ghSMART, we've made in-house referrals a key part not only of our staffing policies but also of promotions. Principals have to source three candidates who can pass a phone screen by our CEO to earn eligibility for a promotion to partner. The payoff, as far as we're concerned, has been little short of amazing. In the past two years, 80 percent of our new hires have come from team member referrals.

Our approach is highly disciplined—we think we should practice what we preach—but virtually any size organization can achieve much the same effect by building internal sourcing into their employee scorecards. Try including something along the lines of "Source [number] A Player candidates per year," then reward the effort by providing a financial or other incentive such as extra vacation time for those who achieve and exceed the goal. Like us, you will quickly find yourself fishing in a greatly enriched pond.

Maybe the greatest benefit of in-house sourcing, though, is how it alters the mind-set throughout an enterprise. By turning employees into talent spotters, everyone starts viewing the business through a *who* lens, not just a *what* one. And why shouldn't they? Ultimately, the organization's fortunes are going to rise or fall on the ability to bring the best people on board. Hold employees accountable for sourcing people through their networks, and everyone will benefit when talent flows into the business.

DEPUTIZING FRIENDS OF THE FIRM

Back in the Wild West days when the marshal was getting ready to head out into the backcountry to hunt down a pack of villains, he would round up a handful of the town's leading citizens, deputize them as temporary law officers, and off the posse would go, riding into the sunset. Law enforcement has grown considerably more sophisticated in the years since, but the idea of extending the reach of your search through "deputizing" some of the most influential people in your network is still a good one.

One company we know offers recruiting bonuses to its deputies—rewards of up to $5,000 if the company hires somebody the deputy sourced, depending on the level of the hire. Other companies provide incentives to their deputies and turn them into unofficial recruiters with gift certificates, iPods, and other valuable items.

BSMB, a multibillion-dollar buyout fund based in New York, has purposefully built an extensive network of deputies to help it source people for its portfolio. John Howard, the company's CEO, described the network to us this way: "We have a group of people who are affiliated with us to whom we can reach out at any time. We have senior executives with all kinds of expertise, so we always have people to call when we need to find A Players in specific industries or to solve certain problems."

In this case, Howard said, the incentive is both particular to the business and quite inventive: "They get to invest in our funds without fees." With BSMB funds typically generating 30 percent or greater annual returns, deputies are quick to return Howard's calls.

Many early-stage companies set up an advisory board to serve the same purpose as BSMB's deputies. These advisors neither involve themselves with governance of the company nor take on fiduciary responsibility. Their reason for being is to offer advice and make introductions. In return, the company rewards them with a small amount of stock or modest cash compensation.

WHI Capital Partners has built both a network and multiple advisory boards to source talent for the companies in its portfolio. As Eric Cohen, a managing partner at the firm, told us, "To date, we have not used any recruiters to hire the five CEOs and ten other high-level executives in our portfolio. We do it a few ways. We bring people in through a trusted network. For example, we are partnered with an organization of two hundred CEOs. We can rely on their recommendations sometimes. We have also built strong boards and advisory boards at our portfolio companies as well as for WHI Capital.

We've been able to find the person just going through a pretty extensive networking process.

"It's kind of like dating. If you are introduced to someone randomly in a bar, there is a chance it might work out, but you are more likely to have a higher success rate if you have a friend or family member introduce you."

Deputizing friends of the firm will create new, accelerated sources of talent, but you still need to pay attention to process, and you have to be disciplined. Make sure that the deputies are reporting in on a regular basis, and whatever incentive you choose, check and double-check that it's sufficient so that busy people will participate.

Remember, you want your recommendations to come from A Players. As the old playground taunt goes, it takes one to know one.

HIRING EXTERNAL RECRUITERS

Recruiters remain a key source for executive talent, but they can do only so much if you don't expose them to the inner culture and workings of your business. Think of recruiters much the way you would think of a doctor or a financial advisor. The more you keep them in the dark about who you are, what's wrong, and what you really need, the less effective they will be.

As the SVP of human resources for Allied Waste, the $6 billion waste management company, Ed Evans has worked with many recruiters throughout his career and has experienced a wide variety of performance levels.

"You have to treat them like partners. Give them enough of a peek under the kimono so they really understand who you are as a firm and as a person. Recruiters who do not understand who you are will be counterproductive."

In fact, great recruiters are unlikely to accept an assignment from you unless they have an opportunity to get that view. Even if they do sign on, they might force you to explore different candidates and perspectives as a way for them to peek under the kimono.

That's part of what the best of the breed do. They educate you about the market for talent, much as a real-estate agent might take you around to multiple houses to gauge your tastes. Being open at the outset, sharing your scorecard, and doing everything else you can to bring an outside recruiter inside both streamlines the process and enhances the results.

HIRING RECRUITING RESEARCHERS

External recruiting firms often contract with recruiting researchers to explore a market, identify sources of talent, and feed names back to the recruiting firm. You can do the same by hiring researchers to augment your sourcing efforts. Researchers won't conduct interviews themselves. Instead, they'll identify names for your internal recruiting team or managers to pursue.

The benefits of this concept are obvious. For minimal cost, companies get a pipeline that taps into a rich source of talent. Even better, hiring the researchers on a contract basis helps maintain a variable cost structure.

The downside with researchers is that they won't qualify candidates as thoroughly as you might like. That vetting process falls on the internal recruiters or the hiring manager directly.

An emphasis on quantity over quality can also clog the hiring process with warm bodies. One company we know was so overwhelmed with the inbound flow of candidates that it finally asked its researchers to screen candidates a little more thoroughly. This reduced the flow of people but increased their value.

You can help tailor the flow of candidates to your needs by taking time at the front end to orient recruiting researchers to your culture, business needs, and even management style and preferences. Unlike external executive recruiters, researchers aren't likely to become your new best friend, but the more they know going in, the more you will get out of them at the end.

SOURCING SYSTEMS

Sourcing talent through these proven practices is easy. The challenge is less a matter of knowing what to do than of putting a system in place to manage the process—and having the discipline to follow through.

When the crunch is on, you and your hiring team are likely to be meeting people all day long, every day. Many of them could be A Players for some role in your company. If you've brought in recruiters and recruiting researchers, they will be bringing still more people to your attention. How do you capture all these names and, more important, follow up with them to build a relationship?

One executive we know uses index cards, and he is methodical in the extreme. Along with their name, he writes down a few snippets he learned, such as a spouse's name or a hobby or a topic of discussion. He routinely revisits these cards and follows up with the people on them. Those who know him marvel at how well he remembers details about their lives.

If you are used to operating in a more high-tech environment, spreadsheets have the added advantage of letting you sort by name and date. Another executive we know generates a weekly call list by loading a follow-up date against every name in his spreadsheet.

Many big companies use off-the-shelf tracking systems to sort and filter job candidates and applicants. We are not in the business of recommending particular vendors. Suffice it to say that a good system will enable all of the employees in your business to contribute names and other useful information to the company's database of potential A Player candidates.

Don't be lulled into inattention by the technology, though. The most high-tech tracking system in the world won't do you any good if you don't use it on a systematic basis. The final step in the sourcing process, the one that matters more than anything else you can do, is scheduling thirty minutes on your calendar every week to identify and nurture A Players. A standing meeting on Monday or Friday will keep you honest by forcing you to call the top talent on your radar screen.

Here's a best practice that puts that thirty minutes to work. Close the door to your office or go into a conference room.

Pull out your list of potential A Players and sort the list by priority. Now, start making calls until you have at least one live conversation.

The conversation does not have to be long. We frequently begin with something simple like, "Sue recommended that you and I connect. I understand you are great at what you do. I am always on the lookout for talented people and would love the chance to get to know you. Even if you are perfectly content in your current job, I'd love to introduce myself and hear about your career interests."

Most people will be thrilled to chat. Done well, you will find you can connect with forty or more new people per year. That's a quick way to build an impressive network.

One more thing. When you are done with the call, assuming you were even moderately impressed with what you heard, be sure to ask the key follow-up question: "Now that you know a little about me, who are the most talented people *you* know who might be a good fit for my company?"

Hiring needs always ebb and flow with the business, but simple systems and disciplines—and simple questions such as the one just shown—will enable your sourcing network to grow exponentially over time.

CASE STUDY: FINDING THE RIGHT CEO

Bank One board members James Crown and John Hall put all these sourcing principles to work when they recruited Jamie Dimon to lead the financial conglomerate, widely regarded as one of the most successful CEO recruitments in recent history.

A little background first. Bank One could trace its roots back to 1868 in Columbus, Ohio, but it was decidedly a creation of the merger mania of the 1980s. In 1988, the bank acquired First Chicago/NBD for $28.9 billion, moved its headquarters to Chicago, and set about trying to merge the two organizations at the corporate headquarters level. The practice, though, was not always perfect.

"In the summer of 1999," Crown told us, "we had serious problems at one of our credit card businesses, First USA. They told us they were going to have a serious earnings shortfall and a significant increase in loan losses. Moreover, the forecast trends were for things to get worse.

"We were clearly headed for trouble, as First USA had been an important source of earnings. No one had confidence that we understood how bad things might be, what we should do, or who would take control of the situation.

"This aggravated an environment that was already tense; neither the board nor the senior management group was truly integrated and working as a team. There had been disagreements about strategy, personnel, and compensation. The stress of impending losses and an eroding balance sheet just made matters worse.

"When John McCoy, the chairman and CEO, left, a treaty was worked out to search for a new CEO to lead the bank. The chairman of the nominating committee and I went on a mission starting in December 1999 to find ourselves a new CEO."

The search committee began by creating a basic score-card—perhaps too basic, Crown said. "We established criteria, but they seemed quite generic: experience, strong general management skills, knowledge of regulation, ability to deal with shareholders and a lot of employees. You write all of these things down because it is a wish list, but you are not really sure what all of these mean."

Next, the Bank One board began searching for a recruiter who could help it find the right person given the complexities of the situation. They finally settled on Andrea Redmond at Russell Reynolds.

Redmond began by working extensively with the board to refine its generic scorecard into something actionable.

"The search consultant has to speak with every board member and feed what she hears back to the whole board to confirm what she heard. You don't want to get down to the wire and realize that board members are on the wrong page. With Bank One, we knew that we needed financial services and we needed leadership—execution style. They were not integrated."

Next, Redmond began sourcing candidates and evaluating additional candidates that the board knew from its networks. Then she put James Crown and John Hall, the chairman of the nominating committee, to work.

"John and I traveled to many locations," Crown recalled. "We met people who were not even interested. We took no as an opening bid. We explored two issues with the candidates: (1) the status of the bank and what they thought was needed, and (2) other candidate names—to learn about people we might not have considered or to source reference checks on the people on our list."

That search process led them finally to Jamie Dimon, who recalled vividly his first meeting with Crown and Hall.

"Jim was a very decent human being. John was a first-class mensch. I told them, 'You don't know me very well. This is like a marriage. I'm going to tell you who I am and what I'm like, and if you don't think I'm the right person, you don't want me.' "

Dimon showed even greater openness in his first session with Andrea Redmond.

"When I first met Jamie, what I was most impressed by was how blatantly candid he was," she recalled. "I'll never forget this. When I am busy and stressed, I can be really abrupt. We sit down. I said, trying to be sensitive, 'So tell me a little bit about your leaving Citigroup.' He said, 'You know what? I was fired.' I was stunned because nobody has ever said that to me. Nobody in fifteen years has come right out and said that. They say something else, like strategic differences, yadda, yadda, yadda. My head flew back. Finally somebody was being totally honest."

Dimon had been a longtime protégé of Sandy Weill at Citigroup, but conflicts arose during their final years together that resulted in his termination. Long viewed as a rising star on Wall Street, Dimon was given many offers.

Still, his forthrightness went a long way toward convincing Redmond, Crown, Hall, and ultimately the Bank One board that Dimon was the right person for the job, and events have borne out that decision time and again. Under Dimon's leadership, Bank One doubled in value and went on to merge with JPMorgan Chase in July 2004, at which point Dimon became

HOW TO SOURCE

1. **REFERRALS FROM YOUR PROFESSIONAL AND PERSONAL NETWORKS.** Create a list of the ten most talented people you know and commit to speaking with at least one of them per week for the next ten weeks. At the end of each conversation, ask, "Who are the most talented people you know?" Continue to build your list and continue to talk with at least one person per week.

2. **REFERRALS FROM YOUR EMPLOYEES.** Add sourcing as an outcome on every scorecard for your team. For example, "Source five A Players per year who pass our phone screen." Encourage your employees to ask people in their networks, "Who are the most talented people you know whom we should hire?" Offer a referral bonus.

3. **DEPUTIZING FRIENDS OF THE FIRM.** Consider offering a referral bounty to select friends of the firm. It could be as inexpensive as a gift certificate or as expensive as a significant cash bonus.

4. **HIRING RECRUITERS.** Use the method described in this book to identity and hire A Player recruiters. Build a scorecard for your recruiting needs, and hold the recruiters you hire accountable for the items on that scorecard. Invest time to ensure the recruiters understand your business and culture.

5. **HIRING RESEARCHERS.** Identify recruiting researchers whom you can hire on contract, using a scorecard to specify your requirements. Ensure they understand your business and culture.

6. **SOURCING SYSTEMS.** Create a system that (1) captures the names and contact information on everybody you source and (2) schedules weekly time on your calendar to follow up. Your solution can be as simple as a spreadsheet or as complex as a candidate tracking system integrated with your calendar.

president and chief operating officer and subsequently CEO and president of JPMorgan Chase at the end of 2005, and chairman of the board a year later.

Why was this search so successful? Part of it was the collaborative working relationship Redmond established with the board. Just as important was the commitment Hall and Crown made to the search process.

"John Hall committed 100 percent of his time to the search," Redmond told us. "He saw eight to twelve candidates. He was very involved and very responsive. When you have a chairman that is willing to make it that kind of priority, you can make it happen."

That commitment, in turn, played a major role in convincing Dimon to sign on to what he knew would be an extremely challenging task. "The board made me feel that I was a high-priority candidate. It takes a lot of trust to take a job like this. The board's personal high involvement level and their flexibility on the issues that were important to me were some of the reasons I took the job."

The larger lessons to be taken away here are the ones we've been stressing throughout this chapter. Take the time to hire and educate the right recruiter. Make sure she understands your needs and culture, and don't miss the opportunity to learn from her. Source from everywhere you can, including the board's network. And stay engaged: If you don't own the process, no one will. Talent is what you need. Focus and commitment will get you there.

FOUR

SELECT
The Four Interviews for Spotting A Players

Steve Kerr, the chief learning officer for Goldman Sachs and former head of GE's learning center, believes that the common interview processes are "almost a random predictor" of job performance. Our research bears that out. According to the four thousand studies and meta-analyses we've examined, traditional interviewing is simply not predictive of job performance.

How, then, do you winnow the candidates that you have found through referrals or that your recruiters and researchers have identified? The best and surest way we have found to select A Players is through a series of four interviews that build

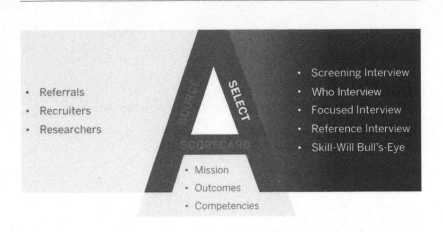

on each other. Collectively, these interviews provide the facts you need to rate a person against the scorecard you have developed for the role. The A Players you want will be those who have a track record that matches your needs, competencies that align with your culture and the role, and plenty of passion to do the job you envision.

To be a great interviewer, you must get out of the habit of passively witnessing how somebody acts *during* an interview. That puts you back in the realm of voodoo hiring methods, where you end up basing your decision on how somebody acts during a few minutes of a certain day. The time span is too limited to reliably predict anything useful. Instead, the four interviews use the time to collect *facts and data about somebody's performance track record that spans decades.*

The four interviews are:

- The screening interview
- The Who Interview™

- The focused interview
- The reference interview

We begin as the sequence begins: with the screening interview.

THE SCREENING INTERVIEW: CULLING THE LIST

The screening interview is a short, phone-based interview designed to clear out B and C Players from your roster of candidates.

To tell the truth, we used to shortchange this front end of the interviewing process. Our clients, though, kept reporting that they were spending too much time conducting subsequent interviews with people who never should have survived the first interview cut. We took that lesson to heart, and in the years since, we've spent a great deal of energy honing our approach to the screening interview to ensure that it yields intended results.

The goal here is to save time by eliminating people who are inappropriate for the position as quickly as possible. We recommend that you conduct the screening interview by phone and that you take no more than thirty minutes. Inviting candidates to your office or out to lunch is sure to gobble up an hour or more of your time.

As with all the interviews we present with the $\underline{A}$ Method, we advocate a structured approach to screening interviews.

> **Screening Interview Guide**
>
> 1. What are your career goals?
>
> 2. What are you really good at professionally?
>
> 3. What are you not good at or not interested in doing professionally?
>
> 4. Who were your last five bosses, and how will they each rate your performance on a 1–10 scale when we talk to them?

This means following a common set of questions *every* time you screen somebody. The commonality fosters consistency and accelerates your ability to discern differences between candidates. Plus, it is just plain easier to know what to ask when you get on the phone with somebody. Why make up questions every time? There is no need to reinvent the wheel.

Four essential questions will help you build a comprehensive fact base for weeding out clear B and C Players in a screening interview.

What are your career goals?

This first question is powerful because it allows you to hear about a candidate's goals and passions before you taint the discussion with your own comments. You give the candidate the first word, rather than telling the person about the company so he or she can parrot back what you just said.

Ideally, a candidate will share career goals that match your company's needs. If he or she lacks goals or sounds like an echo of your own Web site, screen the person out. You are done with the call. Talented people know what they want to do and are not afraid to tell you about it.

You also want to hear the candidate speak with passion and energy about topics that are aligned with the role. A clear misalignment should put you on alert. No matter how talented or qualified a candidate might be, someone who wants to be a manager is not going to be happy if you are trying to hire an individual contributor. Pass the name along to one of your colleagues if some other role in the company seems right for an able candidate, but don't waste any more time considering him or her for the original position.

What are you really good at professionally?

This second question always generates plenty of dialogue. You won't have any trouble getting people to list their strengths. We suggest you push candidates to tell you eight to twelve positives so you can build a complete picture of their professional aptitude. Ask them to give you examples that will put their strengths into context. If they say they are decisive, press for an example of a time when this trait served them well, and remember, you are listening for strengths that match the job at hand. If you see a major gap between someone's strengths and your scorecard, screen that person out.

What are you not good at or not interested in doing professionally?

The third question captures the other side of the balance sheet. You could ask for weaknesses outright, but too often that approach yields cookie-cutter, self-serving answers like "I am impatient for results" or "I work too hard." Instead, let the candidates answer as they will. Then if you're not satisfied, push them for a real weakness or a real area for development. If you hear these cookie-cutter answers, simply say, "That sounds like a strength to me. What are you *really* not good at or not interested in doing?" Talented people will catch the hint and reconsider their responses.

If you still find yourself struggling, we recommend that you put the fear of the reference check into the person. You say, "If you advance to the next step in our process, we will ask for your help in setting up some references with bosses, peers, and subordinates. Okay?" The candidate will say, "Okay." Then you say, "So I'm curious. What do you think *they* will say are some things you are not good at, or not interested in?" Now you'll get an honest and full answer. The thought that you will be talking to references and verifying the candidate's answers compels the candidate to be much more truthful and complete than usual. You will be amazed how much of a truth serum this technique can be at this stage of the screening interview.

Your balance sheet on a candidate will be incomplete if you can't identify at least five to eight areas where a person falls short, lacks interest, or doesn't want to operate. If you come up woefully short, if the weaknesses are all strengths in disguise, or if you see any deal killers relative to your scorecard, then screen the candidate out.

Who were your last five bosses, and how will they each rate your performance on a 1–10 scale when we talk to them?

Notice the language used in the question: "How will they rate you *when* we talk to them?" Not "*if* we talk to them." *When.* Candidates will be thinking, "Uh-oh, I'd better be honest. I can't say my boss would give me a 10 when I really think he'll say 4. Maybe I can get away with saying 5, but that is about it." In our experience, that slight nuance to the question is key to unlocking the truth.

Ask candidates to list each boss and offer a rating for each. Follow up by pressing for details. What makes them think their boss would rate them a 7? Candidates will reinforce and expand upon the list of strengths and weaknesses they gave you in response to the first two questions.

You are looking for lots of 8's, 9's, and 10's in the ratings. Consider 7's neutral; 6's and below are actually bad. We have found that people who give themselves a rating of 6 or lower are really saying 2. If you hear too many 6's and below, screen them out, but be sure to really listen to what is being said. If recruiter Andrea Redmond had pulled the plug on Jamie Dimon because he insisted he was "fired" at Citigroup, Bank One never would have come up with such a dynamic new leader.

Review the scorecard before the call to refresh your memory. Then begin the call by setting expectations, saying something like this: "I am really looking forward to our time together. Here's what I'd like to do. I'd like to spend the first twenty minutes of our call getting to know you. After that, I am happy to answer any questions you have so you can get to know us. Sound good?"

Candidates will almost always agree to that plan. If they are interested enough in the job to talk with you, they'll go with whatever you propose. Now you can launch right into the screening interview questions.

If you don't like what you are hearing, simply collapse the call by accelerating your questions. We regularly finish calls in fifteen to twenty minutes if the initial responses aren't positive. On the other hand, if you hear a strong potential match to your scorecard, you can always ask the candidate if he or she has more time or is willing to schedule more. While you don't want to waste time with the wrong people, you want to make all the time necessary for the right ones.

Conclude the call by offering the candidate an opportunity to ask questions of you. You'll be in a better position to sell the candidate on the virtues of your firm based on what you learned in the first twenty minutes of the call, assuming you liked what you heard. Otherwise, again, you can keep your answers short and collapse that part of the call. Remember, you own the process: you can expand or contract the time you allot based on how well the data you gathered in the call fit the scorecard.

After conducting the interview, ask yourself, "Do this person's strengths match my scorecard? Are the weaknesses manageable? Am I thrilled about bringing this person in for a series of interviews based on the data I have?" You want to be excited about that possibility. You want to have the feeling that you have found *the one*. If you have any hesitation, or if you find yourself thinking you want to bring candidates in just to test them a little more, then screen them out. Only invite in those whose profile appears to be a strong match for your scorecard.

GETTING CURIOUS: WHAT, HOW, TELL ME MORE

The screening interview questions are simple to remember and easy to administer. That's one of the beauties of the A Method. But unless you follow up on the four primary questions, you won't get all the answers you need.

There are literally thousands of additional questions you could ask. Rather than create a screening guide that tries to cover all the possibilities, we use a simple process called "getting curious." Here's how it works. After a candidate answers one of the primary questions above, get curious about the answer by asking a follow-up question that begins with "What," "How," or "Tell me more." Keep using this framework until you are clear about what the person is really saying.

For example, suppose you just asked someone the third screening interview question—"What are you not good at or not interested in doing professionally?"—and the candidate replied, "I am not great at dealing with conflict."

The fact is, not dealing with conflict can mean a lot of different things. Does the candidate cower when under attack? Does he run for the hills? Or does he live in the hills so that he never gets attacked? Here's a chance to get curious using the "What? How? Tell me more" framework. Let's see how this particular conversation might play out.

"*What* do you mean?" you ask.

"I mean I am conflict-avoidant."

"*How* so?" you ask again.

"Well, I guess I avoid situations where I know people are going to get upset."

"*What* is an example of that?"

"There was this one time where I had two employees who were not getting along. One guy had a habit of yelling at this woman. I had a hard time dealing with that."

"*How* did you deal with it?" you ask.

"I finally pulled him aside and told him that he had to stop. He didn't, so I pulled him aside again and told him I would have to fire him if he did it again."

"*What* happened?"

"He did it again."

"*Tell me more.*"

"He blew up at this poor woman for not shipping the right product to a key customer. I felt really bad for her."

"*What* did you do?"

"I pulled him aside again and repeated my threat to fire him."

"*How* did that feel?"

"Terrible. I didn't sleep for a week leading up to the conversation. I felt like I was getting an ulcer."

"*What* happened next?"

"Nothing. He calmed down on his own. Then I was transferred out of the department a month later, so I got lucky. I didn't have to deal with it."

Notice how simple these questions are. None of them is longer than six words. They all begin with "What," "How," or "Tell me more." They all play off the previous statement the candidate made. And look at what we learned about this poor fellow. Would you hire him for a key management job where a lot of change was needed? The "What? How? Tell me more" framework is completely open-ended when it comes to asking follow-up questions. Sample questions include: What do you mean? What did that look like? What happened? What is a good example of that? What was your role? What did you do? What did your boss say? What were the results? What else? How did you do that? How did that go? How did you feel? How much money did you save? How did you deal with that?

Sure, it can seem like you are probing a lot, but this is a key step in an important *who* decision that can affect your entire company. You should be pushing candidates to be as clear and precise as possible by asking "what" and "how" questions. When you have no idea what else to ask, just say, "Tell me more." They will keep talking. We promise.

HIT THE GONG FAST

The whole point of the screening interview is to weed people out as quickly as possible. We mentioned that before, but it bears repeating.

The 1970s TV phenomenon *The Gong Show,* the forerunner of many of today's so-called reality shows, provides a nice model for screening interviews. Contestants competed for what then seemed like fabulous trips and prizes by displaying a broad and highly variable array of talents. It usually didn't take long for the panel of judges to recognize the duds. As soon as it became clear that a contestant lacked any talent whatsoever, one of the judges would stand up, do a little dance, and hit a giant gong. Contestants were whisked off-stage before they could complain, while gleeful audiences celebrated or booed the judge's decision.

It wasn't always pretty, but in fact hitting the gong fast is exactly what good screening is all about. Too many managers make the costly mistake of lingering with candidates who are a bad match. Some are simply avoiding confrontation. Others think, "If I have my colleagues Janet, Rick, and Charlotte interview this person, they'll see something I don't." That might sound collegial, but you are just wasting everybody's time. Better to miss out on a potential A Player than to waste precious hours on a borderline case that turns out to be a B or C Player.

Adam Meyers, chief executive for the Health Optics and Photonics Division of Halma PLC, taught us the importance of this lesson from his own experience.

"My team and I didn't pay much attention to the screening interview when we first started using your system. We did them, but we weren't rigorous enough. We found we were spending far too much time with people we had brought in for the day who were clearly not a fit. We should have known better. We wasted a lot of time."

Meyers encouraged his team to screen more aggressively.

Today, only 10–20 percent of the people they talk to on the phone pass their rigorous screening interview.

"My team spends much less time with the wrong people," Meyers said. "That enables them to spend more time with the right people. It is a much more efficient process." And a far more productive one, too. By screening out those who are clearly B and C Players for a particular role, Halma can spend more time with those most likely to be A Players.

John Sharpe offers another perspective on screening. He spent twenty-three years at Four Seasons Hotels and Resorts, most recently as president. "I think gut feel and instinct is particularly important in determining who *not* to hire," he told us. "I don't think you can hire based on gut feel alone. You have to examine their record. But when everything looks good on paper, if you have a gnawing feeling that you don't feel comfortable with the person, or if you don't totally trust the person, then you should pass."

Sharpe told us about a time when a small data point he observed reversed all of the positive information known about a candidate.

"There was this candidate for a key management position in the company, not in my group," he said. "We were on a plane from Toronto to Texas. This guy told the flight attendant that he had only Canadian money, but I saw he had U.S. dollars in his wallet, too. He was winking to me and buying drinks with Canadian money, which at the time the airlines would just count on a one-for-one basis even though the U.S. dollar was 30 percent stronger.

"I did not feel comfortable with this deceit. Somebody else in our company hired him. Once he was on the job, he treated the front-line people without respect and went back on commitments that were made to them. He was fired within two months. In this case, the gut picked up on something important that did not show up in any resumes, interviews, or references."

The screening interview will allow you to quickly narrow the list of candidates to a small handful that you want to pursue further. Once you have your narrowed list of two to five candidates, you can wheel out the heavy interviewing artillery.

THE WHO INTERVIEW:
THE POWER OF PATTERNS FOR CHOOSING *WHO*

Screening interviews separate the wheat from the chaff, but they are not precise enough to ensure a 90 percent or better hiring success rate. To be more confident and accurate in your selection, you will want to conduct a Who Interview.

The Who Interview is the key interview within the "Select" step of the ghSMART A Method for Hiring. It goes a long way toward giving you confidence in your selection because it uncovers the patterns of somebody's career history, which you can match to your scorecard.

This style of interviewing is the most valid and reliable predictor of performance, according to a half-century's worth of thousands of research studies in the field of industrial psychol-

* Smart, B.D. & Smart, G.H. (1997). Topgrading the Organization. Directors & Boards, Spring, p22-28.

† Topgrading is a registered trademark of Topgrading, Inc. All rights reserved.

ogy. One of the early pioneers in the field is Brad Smart, Geoff's father. Brad and Geoff coauthored the 1997 article "Topgrading the Organization." Brad went on to write the book *Topgrading*, which describes his approach to talent management.

In a conversation with us, Brad Smart explained how he came to use this type of interview over thirty years ago.

"After completing my doctoral work, I went to work with a group of management psychologists for a couple of years where I conducted management interviews. I was barely twenty-five years old and felt insecure about not having much job experience. So I figured I might as well ask a lot more questions than what was typical.

"I sat in on one interview with a senior partner. He conducted a one-hour interview and asked if I had any additional questions to ask. I took the candidate back to my cube and started asking him more questions. A lot more. He told me all sorts of stories about his career successes and failures as we walked through his career. Later, the senior partner compared my report to his and said that his report was terrible compared to the report I had just done. His spoke in generalities, while mine was full of facts and stories that supported my conclusions."

What Brad Smart discovered was the power of using data and patterns of behavior for making predictions about how somebody is likely to perform in the future.

"The patterns become clearer and clearer," he told us, "so it becomes easy to get a fix on exactly what the individual's strengths and weaknesses are today. It discloses the likelihood that a person will improve on strengths or minimize weaker

---

Who Interview Guide

1. What were you hired to do?

2. What accomplishments are you most proud of?

3. What were some low points during that job?

4. Who were the people you worked with? Specifically:

    i.   What was your boss's name, and how do you spell that? What was it like working with him/her? What will he/she tell me were your biggest strengths and areas for improvement?

    ii. How would you rate the team you inherited on an A, B, C scale? What changes did you make? Did you hire anybody? Fire anybody? How would you rate the team when you left it on an A, B, C scale?

5. Why did you leave that job?

---

points. If the pattern is there of extracting success out of the jaws of defeat, that makes you want to hire somebody."

Matt Levin of Bain Capital put it this way: "Boards make mistakes when they don't take the time to learn the story of the person. Everybody has strengths and weaknesses. If you want to enhance your predictive capabilities, you have to really understand their story and their patterns."

So what is the Who Interview? It's a chronological walk-through of a person's career. You begin by asking about the highs and lows of a person's educational experience to gain insight into his or her background. Then you ask five simple questions, for each job in the past fifteen years, beginning with the earliest and working your way forward to the present day.

These five questions are so straightforward that the discussion they generate seems more like a conversation than an interview. Boards and CEOs find this attractive because they can interview senior executives without the process feeling like some kind of interrogation. People being interviewed enjoy it because they feel like they are just telling their story. And everybody likes talking about their favorite subject (themselves) for as long as they have a willing listener! What you are really doing, though, is gathering an immense amount of decision data points.

The WHO Interview

What were you hired to do?

This first question is a clear window into candidates' goals and targets for a specific job. In a way, you are trying to discover what their scorecard might have been if they had had one. They might not know off the top of their head, so coach them by asking how they thought their success was measured in the role. Build a mental image of what their scorecard should have been. What were their mission and key outcomes? What competencies might have mattered?

What accomplishments are you most proud of?

Question number two generates wonderful discussions about the peaks of a person's career. This is where you will hear the stories behind the polished statements on a resume. In our experience, most candidates naturally focus on what really mattered to them at that time in their career rather than regurgitate what they put on their resume.

Ideally, candidates will tell you about accomplishments that match the job outcomes they just described to you. Even better, those accomplishments will match the scorecard for the position you are trying to fill.

On the flip side, we are always wary when a candidate's accomplishments seem to lack any correlation to the expectations of the job. Be sure to listen for that clue. A Players tend to talk about outcomes linked to expectations. B and C Players talk generally about events, people they met, or aspects of the job they liked without ever getting into results.

What were some low points during that job?

People can be hesitant to share their lows at first, opting instead to say something like, "I didn't have any lows. Those were good years! Yup, those were good years, I tell you!" The disclaimers are understandable, but there isn't a person alive who can seriously make this claim. Everybody, and we mean *everybody*, has work lows.

Our recommendation is to reframe the question over and over until the candidate gets the message. "What went really wrong? What was your biggest mistake? What would you have done differently? What part of the job did you not like? In what ways were your peers stronger than you?" Don't let the candidate off the hook. Keep pushing until the candidate shares the lows.

Who were the people you worked with?

Question four builds on the fourth question of the screening interview. Brad Smart calls the first part TORC, or threat of reference check. This is one part of the interview where the precision and order of the questions really matter. To get the best results, follow the questions exactly.

Begin by asking candidates for their boss's name. Ask them to spell it for you, and make a point to show them you are writing it down. "John Smith, you say? That is *S, M, I, T, H,* right?" Forcing candidates to spell the name out no matter how common it might be sends a powerful message: you *are* going to call, so they should tell the truth.

Next, ask what they thought it was like working with John Smith. At the positive extreme, you will hear people offer high praise for their bosses and how they received mentoring and coaching from them over the years. A neutral answer will sound somewhat more reserved without being particularly positive or negative.

At the negative extreme, people tell you that one boss was useless, the next was a jerk, and the third a complete moron. Oddly, some candidates fail to make the connection that they are talking to their potential new boss—you. What colorful name will *you* earn if you hire this person? Being called a moron might be the least of your problems.

Now ask, "What will Mr. Smith say were your biggest strengths and areas for improvement?" Be sure to say *will*, not *would*. This is like the spelling question above. By asking "What *will* Mr. Smith say?" you are again signaling that this isn't a hypothetical question. You mean business. Candidates quickly realize they have to tell you the truth because you are going to learn it from your reference calls anyway.

Another wonderful principle is at work here: reciprocity. Reciprocity is like a catalyst to the truth serum. Geoff once was walking with his wife and kids by a store that sold cowboy hats. Out front, the owner was grilling hotdogs. "Want a hotdog?" he asked Geoff, who stopped and said, "Yes, thank you." "Would they like one too?" the owner asked Geoff, loud enough for all of his children to hear. "Yeah!" the kids replied in unison. You know what happens next in the story. Geoff got a few free hotdogs, but thirty minutes later found himself walking out of the store with cowboy hats for each of his family members. That's the principle of reciprocity.

That same reciprocity applies to TORC. The candidate has just spent two minutes telling you about John Smith with perfect clarity. Now he owes you two minutes on what Mr. Smith will say about him. The human brain wants to balance out the equation, so the adjectives that describe the strengths and weaknesses will spill out of your candidate's mouth as he steps into Mr. Smith's shoes.

Nothing, of course, works every time. Some candidates will insist that they don't know what the boss will say. Our advice is to keep reframing the question until you get an answer, but even that can take unusual persistence.

ghSMART consultant Christian Zabbal once had a particularly stubborn candidate who pushed Zabbal's reframing skills to the limit. Zabbal asked him what his boss was going to say when he spoke with him, and the candidate said he didn't know. So Zabbal reframed the question.

"What is your best guess for what he will say?" he asked again.

"I don't know," the candidate replied.

"What kind of feedback did he give you on your reviews?" Zabbal tried again.

"He never gave me any reviews," he said flatly.

"What about informally? What did he tell you in passing?"

"He never told me anything. He never came out of his office long enough to give me any feedback."

"Well, what do you think he told others when he talked about you behind your back in his office, maybe to the board?" Zabbal was exhausting his repertoire of follow-up questions.

The candidate paused for a moment after this last question, then said, "You know what, that is a good question. My buddies and I got so tired of not knowing what he was doing in that office of his that we finally snuck in one night and bugged it. We knew he was going to have a meeting the next day to talk about us with the board. We listened to the whole conversation."

Zabbal was in shock at what he had just heard, but he wanted to keep the candidate talking. He put on the straightest face he could muster and asked, "So what did he say about you?"

We rest our case. There is always a better answer than "I don't know." Sometimes it might really surprise you! TORC has a way of uncovering a mother lode of data about a person.

The second part of the fourth question—"How would you rate the team you inherited?"—is applicable to managers. The focus here is on how candidates approach building a strong team. Do they accept the hand they have been dealt when they inherit a new team, or do they make changes to get a better hand? What changes do they make? How long does it take? As a bonus, use the TORC framework on their team. You can ask, "When we speak with members of your team, what *will they* say were your biggest strengths and weaknesses as a manager?"

Why did you leave that job?

The final question of this vital Who Interview can be one of the most insight-producing questions you ask. Were the candidates for your position promoted, recruited, or fired from each job along their career progression? Were they taking the next step in their career or running from something? How did they feel about it? How did their boss react to the news?

A Players are highly valued by their bosses. B and C Players often are not. It is an important piece of the puzzle to figure out if somebody decided to leave a job after being successful (an A Player clue) or whether he or she was pushed out of a job by a boss who did not value their contribution (a B or C Player cluc). A Players perform well, and bosses express disappointment when they quit. B and C Players perform less well and are nudged out of their jobs or forcefully pushed out by their bosses.

Don't accept vague answers like "My boss and I didn't connect." That's a non-answer. Get curious. Find out why, and stick with it until you have clear picture of what actually happened.

We encountered a particularly striking example of the power of this last question when we were interviewing a former VP of sales on behalf of a group of investors who were considering him for a CEO position. In the course of running through a list of his previous jobs, we asked, "Why did you leave that job?"

He replied, "I had a philosophical disagreement with my boss."

That sparked our "What? How? Tell me more" curiosity. "What happened?" we asked.

"Well," he replied, "I guess it came down to this one board meeting. I was there with my CEO, and the board was giving him a hard time because we had fallen short on our sales numbers."

"What were the numbers?" we asked the former VP of sales.

"We were off our goal by 25 percent. The board was not happy. They really had my CEO squirming with all of their questions. He finally cracked under the pressure and said to the board, 'If we do not achieve our target this next quarter, we'll have to get a new VP of sales—meaning *my job*!' "

"What did you do?" we asked, sensing this was about to get interesting.

"Well," he said, "I looked him right in the eye and said, 'You know what? Your mother had a lot of foresight when she named you.' "

Our minds started whirring with the possibilities. There were so many questions we wanted to explore. "What was his name?" we finally asked.

"Well, his given name was Richard, but he went by the common nickname for Richard."

Once again, we fought hard to maintain a straight face. This guy had just insulted his boss, the CEO, in front of the board of directors! "What happened next?" we prodded.

"The board thought it was hysterical, but Richard didn't. He adjourned the meeting for fifteen minutes and called me into his office. That was when he fired me."

Aha! Now we were getting somewhere. But we were still curious. This story was too strange to pass up. "What did you say when he fired you?"

"I said, 'You know what your problem is? Nobody has ever put you in your place.' Then the CEO said to me, 'Who do you think is going to put me in my place? You?'"

A smile crept across our candidate's face. It was a loaded smile because we had learned earlier in his interview that he was most proud of leading his high school hockey team in penalty minutes.

"So what did you do?" we pushed.

"I hit him!"

Now our curiosity was killing us. We couldn't stop ourselves. "How did you hit him, exactly?" we asked.

"It was sort of an open-handed slap across the face, but I hit him pretty hard!"

"What happened then?" We were on the edge of our seats.

"That's when he terminated me with cause. My wife and I like to call it my $3 million slap."

"How so?"

"I had options worth $3 million, which I lost the minute that I, um, er, slapped the CEO."

Ouch.

There wasn't much more we could ask our candidate at this point. What began as a philosophical difference with his boss had ended with a $3 million slap. And the most amazing part of this story is not just what happened but the fact that the VP of sales, *the slapper himself,* revealed it during our interview.

You will be surprised at how often stories like this come up in a Who Interview. That's why we long ago learned to suspend our judgment during the interview and get curious. You never know what you might hear as the picture fills in and the person's true identity is revealed.

CONDUCTING AN EFFECTIVE WHO INTERVIEW

To put the Who Interview into practice, divide a person's career "story" into the equivalent of "chapters." Each chapter could be a single job, or a group of jobs that span three to five years. For example, one candidate our firm interviewed had a thirty-six-page resume. The candidate was an entrepreneur in the music and film businesses as both a performer and a teacher, and listed every project, article, and credit.

ghSMART consultant Michael Haugen spent the first ten

minutes of the interview working with the candidate to divide his resume into eight chapters based on the kind of positions he had held during each phase of his career. It wasn't perfect, but the roles the candidate held in each chapter of three to five years roughly fit together.

Then Haugen asked the five questions above for each of the eight chapters, starting with the earliest set of projects and working his way forward toward present day. We can't stress this enough: the order is important. Don't start at the most recent job and work backward. Candidates can't think clearly that way. Instead, walk through the career history chronologically—as the events really happened. Candidates will settle into telling you their story, and you will get to hear the narrative of their work life unfolding.

The Who Interview takes three hours on average to conduct. It might take five hours for CEOs of multibillion-dollar companies, or ninety minutes for entry-level positions. The ultimate time depends on the length of a person's career and the number of chapters you create.

The length of the interview will help you in two ways initially. First, it will encourage you to get really good at the screening interview so you are able to spend most of your time with the best candidates. Second, it will enable you to reduce your hiring failure rate by such a wide margin that you will never hire another person again without using this methodology.

For every hour you spend in the Who Interview, you'll save hundreds of hours by not dealing with C Players. The return on your time is staggeringly high.

In practical terms, this means that you, the hiring manager (or board member if you are hiring a CEO), will want to conduct the Who Interview yourself. You own the hire. You will suffer the consequences of making a mistake. Your career and job happiness depend on finding A Players. And you want to be in the room when a candidate reveals the hundreds of data points that will enable you to make a great decision.

That said, we also recommend that you conduct the Who Interview with a colleague—perhaps someone from HR, another manager or member of your team, or simply someone who wants to learn the method by observing you. This tandem approach makes it easier to run the interview. One person can ask the questions while the other takes notes, or you can both do a little of each. Either way, two heads are always better than one.

Kick off the interview by setting expectations. Candidates are likely to feel a bit anxious because you will have told them that this interview is going to be different from what they have done in the past, but they won't quite know how it will be different.

Here's a simple script that you can use to set the stage.

> Thank you for taking the time to visit us today. As we have already discussed, we are going to do a chronological interview to walk through each job you have held. For each job I am going to ask you five core questions: What were you hired to do? What accomplishments are you most proud of? What were some low points during that job? Who were the people you worked with? Why did you leave that job?

The WHO Interview

At the end of the interview we will discuss your career goals and aspirations, and you will have a chance to ask me questions.

Eighty percent of the process is in this room, but if we mutually decide to continue, we will conduct reference calls to complete the process.

Finally, while this sounds like a lengthy interview, it will go remarkably fast. I want to make sure you have the opportunity to share your full story, so it is my job to guide the pace of the discussion. Sometimes, we'll go into more depth in a period of your career. Other times, I will ask that we move on to the next topic. I'll try to make sure we leave plenty of time to cover your most recent, and frankly, most relevant jobs.

Do you have any questions about the process?

Setting expectations will put the candidate at ease and enable you to launch into the first chapter of his or her career with minimal confusion or intimidation.

MASTER TACTICS

Now you know the basic Who Interview. After training thousands of managers on this approach, we commonly hear that it is surprisingly easy to do. It is conversational. It is natural. And it delivers immense amounts of relevant data.

However, first time users tend to struggle with the same issues for this approach to interviewing. We have listened to that feedback and offer five master tactics to make the interview as easy and effective as possible.

Master Tactic #1: Interrupting

You have to interrupt the candidate. There is no avoiding it. *You have to interrupt the candidate.* If you don't, he or she might talk for ten hours straight about things that are not at all relevant. It may feel rude to interrupt somebody who is enthusiastically telling you a story about that smelly pig farm in Kentucky that was right next to the corporate offices. However, we think it is rude to let somebody ramble. It hurts their chance of having time to cover important events in their career. So interrupt the person once you think they are going off course. You will have to interrupt the candidate at least once every three or four minutes, so get ready.

There is a bad way and a good way to interrupt somebody during an interview.

The bad way to interrupt somebody is to put up your hand like a stop sign gesture and say, "Wait, wait, wait. Let me stop you there. Can we get back on track?" This shames the candidate, implies that they have done something *wrong,* and makes them clam up for good. You will really struggle to get the person to open up after that.

The good way to interrupt somebody is to smile broadly, match their enthusiasm level, and use reflective listening to get them to stop talking without demoralizing them. You say, "Wow! It sounds like that pig farm next to the corporate office smelled horrible!" The candidate nods and says "Yes!" and appreciates your empathy and respect. Then you immediately say, "You were just telling me about launching that direct mail campaign. I'd *love* to hear what was that like? How well did it go?"

See the difference in rapport? The shut-you-up approach really deflates the candidate's willingness to reveal information to you. The I'm-really-excited-to-hear-more-about-such-and-such approach keeps the rapport high, and gives the candidate a new and more relevant topic to tell you about.

It is through maintaining very high rapport that you get the most valuable data, and polite interrupting can build that rapport.

Master Tactic #2: The Three P's

How do you know if an accomplishment a person tells you about is great, good, okay, or lousy? Use the three P's. The three P's are questions you can use to clarify how valuable an accomplishment was in any context. The questions are:

1. How did your performance compare to the *previous* year's performance? (For example, this person achieved sales of $2 million and the previous year's sales were only $150,000.)
2. How did your performance compare to the *plan*? (For example, this person sold $2 million and the plan was $1.2 million.)
3. How did your performance compare to that of *peers*? (For example, this person sold $2 million and was

ranked first among thirty peers; the next-best per-former sold only $750,000.)

Master Tactic #3: Push Versus Pull

People who perform well are generally pulled to greater op-portunities. People who perform poorly are often pushed out of their jobs. Do not hire anybody who has been pushed out of 20 percent or more of their jobs. From our experience, those folks have a three times higher chance of being a chronic B or C Player.

Here is how to go about judging this. After you ask, "Why did you leave that job?" you will hear one of two answers:

1. *Push.* "It was mutual." "It was time for me to leave." "My boss and I were not getting along." "Judy got promoted and I did not." "My role shrank." "I missed my number and was told I was on thin ice." "I slapped the CEO so hard that I lost my $3 million severance package."
2. *Pull.* "My biggest client hired me." "My old boss re-cruited me to a bigger job." "The CEO asked me to take a double promotion." "A former peer went to a competitor and referred me to his boss."

Master Tactic #4: Painting a Picture

You'll know you understand what a candidate is saying when you can literally see a picture of it in your mind. Ted Bililies, a

The WHO Interview

managing director at ghSMART, calls this ability "empathic imagination." Empathic imagination helps you move away from generic answers that don't mean anything and toward specific details that give you real insight. Wayne Huizenga, the only person in America responsible for listing six companies on the New York Stock Exchange and founding three Fortune 500 companies, put it this way: "You always try to put yourself in someone else's shoes. What happened in the last job? Why did that not work out? You are trying to put yourself in their shoes to understand how and why they are making decisions and handling problems."

For example, a candidate might say she is an excellent communicator. Don't assume you know what that means. Get curious to truly understand. You might learn (1) that she is an exceptional business writer who works on all of her company's newsletters and marketing collateral but (2) that she is also a terrible presenter. Both of these answers offer far more insight into the candidate than a general statement about being a good communicator.

Master Tactic #5: Stopping at the Stop Signs

One of the advantages of conducting the Who Interview in person is that you can watch for shifts in body language and other inconsistencies. An entire science has evolved to tell when people are lying. The biggest indicator, as it turns out, is when you see or hear inconsistencies. If someone says, "We did great in that role," while shifting in his chair, looking down, and covering his mouth, that is a stop sign. When you see that, slam on the brakes, get curious, and see just how "great" he actually did. There is probably more to the story than he wants you to know.

The idea isn't to gather dirt. That's never the point of the Who Interview. If you come off like an investigative reporter or, worse, a gossip columnist, you need to seriously refine your approach. Think of yourself instead as a biographer interviewing a subject. You want both the details and the broad pattern, the facts and texture. That's how you make an informed *who* decision.

THE FOCUSED INTERVIEW: GETTING TO KNOW MORE

The Who Interview is comprehensive and will get you most of the way toward the right answer of *who* to hire. Conduct it in tandem with a colleague, and the two of you will have a rich dataset to work from. In fact, we've seen plenty of great hires made on the basis of this interview alone.

But we recommend one more step, the focused interview, which is leg three of the "Select" step of the ghSMART <u>A</u> Method for Hiring. Focused interviews allow you to gather additional, specific information about your candidate. In essence, you are turning the magnification up another notch so you can give would-be hires one last look with a finer degree of granularity.

These interviews also offer a chance to involve other team members directly in the hiring process. We think there's great value in that, but a few cautions first. Be sure to emphasize to

Focused Interview Guide

1. The purpose of this interview is to talk about_____. (Fill in the blank with a specific outcome or competency, such as the person's experience selling to new customers, building and leading a team, creating strategic plans, acting aggressively and persistently, etc.)

2. What are your biggest accomplishments in this area during your career?

3. What are your insights into your biggest mistakes and lessons learned in this area?

your team that this is *not* meant to be another Who Interview. One time through a candidate's full story is enough. Stress, too, that everyone is to follow the script. Otherwise, some of your colleagues might fall back on their favorite voodoo hiring methods. That's the last thing you need at this point.

The focused interview is similar to the commonly used behavioral interview with one major difference: *it is focused on the outcomes and competencies of the scorecard,* not some vaguely defined job description or manager's intuition. You have a good idea who you want by this point, but you still need to be as certain as you can that candidate and position are a perfect match. The focused interview is, in essence, your odds enhancer.

The questions follow a simple structure, just like the other interviews in the A Method (see box above). We recommend leading with these primary questions to get the conversation started. As with all of the interviews we present in this book, get curious after every answer by using the "What? How? Tell me more" framework, and keep asking until you understand *what* the person did and *how* he or she did it.

For example, let's say you are hiring a VP of sales. The scorecard you created has four outcomes on it:

1. Grow domestic sales from $500 million to $600 million by December 31, and continue growing them by 20 percent per year for the next five years.
2. Maintain at least a 45 percent gross margin across the portfolio of products annually.
3. Hire the sales organization, ensuring 90 percent or more of all new hires are A Players as defined by the sales scorecards. Achieve a 90 percent or better ratio of A Players across the team within three years through hiring and coaching. Remove all chronic C Players within ninety days of identification.
4. Create a sales strategy that the CEO approves during the annual planning cycle.

In addition, let's say you have identified six competencies that define success in the job:

1. Aggressive
2. Persistent
3. Hires A Players
4. Holds people accountable

5. Follows through on commitments
6. Open to criticism and feedback

Try assigning three members of your team to perform focused interviews based on this scorecard. The first interviewer takes the first two outcomes and the first two competencies because they all have to do with growing sales and managing costs, and the behaviors that support both. The second interviewer has responsibility for the outcome related to Who and the two competencies having to do with how the candidate builds the team. That leaves everything else for the third interviewer.

Each interview should take forty-five minutes to one hour, depending on how many outcomes and competencies you assign to each interviewer. Regardless of the time spent, each interviewer will bring supplemental data to your decision-making process.

DOUBLE-CHECKING THE CULTURAL FIT

Focused interviews also give you a final gauge on the cultural fit that so many of our CEOs and other business leaders cited as critical to the hiring process. Just be sure to include competencies and outcomes that go beyond the specifics of the job to embrace the larger values of your company.

First Solar, a rapidly growing maker of solar panels, found itself challenged by its own success. Its growth created a voracious appetite for A Players, but too many of the talented people who got inside the door couldn't handle the fast-paced culture of the company.

To address this challenge, the company created a cultural fit interview based on the focused interview framework. Mike Ahearn, First Solar's CEO, painted the big picture for us. "We are a fast-moving, aggressive company. We need people on our team who will never be satisfied with the status quo. They need to be results-oriented people who work toward continuous improvement. And they have to put safety first, build deep customer relationships, and recognize that people matter. These are our values. This is what we look for. If people don't live by these values, they will never fit with our company."

Carol Campbell, the VP of HR for First Solar, filled in the details. "We conduct at least one cultural fit interview for every candidate, using questions built around our cultural values. We find it works really well after the Who Interview because the two interviews together ensure we hire people who are both capable of getting the job done and able to thrive in the First Solar culture."

Is the interview foolproof? Of course not, but First Solar has made very few hiring mistakes over the past few years, and that track record has paid off big-time. The company recently enjoyed an IPO that far exceeded market expectations. The stock was the top-performing small- and mid-cap equity in the United States in 2007. In Mike Ahearn's words, "Our success could not have happened without the strong team we have assembled."

The FOCUSED Interview

TYPICAL INTERVIEW DAY

8:30 A.M.–8:45 A.M. Team meeting. Bring the interview team together for fifteen minutes at the beginning of the day (or the night before) to review the scorecard, the candidate's resume, notes from the screening interview, and roles and responsibilities for the day.

8:45 A.M.–9:00 A.M. Have a team member greet the candidate on arrival and spend a few minutes orienting him or her to the day, and possibly to the company.

9:00 A.M.–12:00 P.M. Who Interview. The hiring manager and one other colleague conduct a tandem interview that lasts one and a half to three hours, depending on the length of the candidate's career.

12:00 P.M.–1:30 P.M. Lunch. A few team members, preferably not involved in the interview process, take the candidate to lunch. We like to keep this informal—this is a pressure-packed day as it is—but if you or the candidate is pressed for time, you can continue interviewing while you eat.

1:30 P.M.–4:30 P.M. Focused interviews. One to three team members conduct focused interviews based on their assigned portions of the scorecard. (Note: Some companies conduct focused interviews as a second round of interviews only after a candidate passes the Who Interview in an earlier round. This enables them to save time if a candidate does not pass the Who Interview, but it does force them to schedule multiple interview days. Other companies do it all in one day.)

4:30 P.M.–4:45 P.M. Host thanks the candidate and explains next steps.

4:45 P.M.–5:30 P.M. Candidate discussion. Interview team convenes for thirty to sixty minutes at the end of the day to rate the scorecard and develop a list of the candidate's strengths and weaknesses based on the actual data gathered during the day. The hiring manager makes a go/no-go decision at the end of the meeting regarding whether to conduct reference calls or terminate the process.

THE REFERENCE INTERVIEW:
TESTING WHAT YOU LEARNED

The three interviews are over. The data you gathered about your candidate match up perfectly with the job and your culture. She was a hit with your team. In your mind, she already works for you. You may be tempted to skip reference checks and make an offer now.

Don't skip the references!

What can a reference tell you that you and your colleagues haven't already gleaned after that exhausting day of interviews? A lot, it turns out.

Robert Hurst is the retired vice chairman of Goldman Sachs and is currently managing director of Crestview Advisors, a private equity firm. He recalled a story that vividly captures the importance of attending to this last critical step in the hiring process.

"We hired a chief financial officer. We were not allowed to make reference calls because she wanted to keep her candidacy a secret. And she was a disaster. Her problem was she was too used to process and routine. She moved to a place that is more complicated and stressful, and she could not handle the stress. Without having a chance to do reference calls, you lose 25 percent of the information you should know." Hurst won't get fooled again. He has personally conducted reference calls for almost every hire he has made since.

In fact, 64 percent of the business moguls we interviewed conduct reference calls for *every* hire, not just the ones at the top. Unfortunately, far fewer general managers follow suit.

The REFERENCE Interview

Why? Pushback from the candidate is one reason; time constraints are another. Many managers simply write off reference interviews as a waste of time, which is true when the interview is poorly constructed. The answer, though, isn't to drop the interview. The answer is to do it right.

There are three things you have to do to have successful reference interviews.

First, pick the right references. Review your notes from the Who Interview and pick the bosses, peers, and subordinates with whom you would like to speak. Don't just use the reference list the candidate gives you.

Second, ask the candidate to contact the references to set up the calls. Some companies have a policy that prevents employees from serving as references. You may hit that brick wall if you call a reference directly, but we have found that you will have twice the chance of actually getting to talk to a reference if you ask the candidate to set up the interview—whether it is during business hours or after hours at home.

Third, conduct the right number of reference interviews. We recommend that you personally do about four and ask your colleagues to do three, for a total of seven reference interviews. Interview three past bosses, two peers or customers, and two subordinates.

In the $\underline{A}$ Method we ask five simple questions (see box on the following page). Do these questions look familiar? They should. They follow the same structured pattern as the other interviews we recommended. This makes it very easy to merge what you hear with what you have already learned about a candidate.

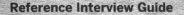

Reference Interview Guide

1. In what context did you work with the person?

2. What were the person's biggest strengths?

3. What were the person's biggest areas for improvement *back then*?

4. How would you rate his/her overall performance in that job on a 1–10 scale? What about his or her performance causes you to give that rating?

5. The person mentioned that he/she struggled with _____ in that job. Can you tell me more about that?

The first question is really a conversation starter and memory jogger. You already know the answer based on your Who Interview, but the people you are calling might need a minute to remember the work they did with the candidate before they can get into the details.

The next two questions are exactly the same as the screening interview ones. In both cases, ask for multiple examples to help you put strengths and development areas into context. And, once again, don't forget to get curious by using the "What? How? Tell me more" framework to clarify responses.

The third question is even more powerful when you add the phrase "back then" to the end of the question: "What were the person's biggest areas for improvement *back then*?" These two words liberate a reference to talk about weaknesses that existed in the past. Surely, they might assume, the person has corrected those weaknesses. At the very least, they can tell

The REFERENCE Interview

themselves that they aren't being critical of the candidate in the present tense. In truth, we believe, people don't change that much. People aren't mutual funds. Past performance really is an indicator of future performance.

Next, ask the reference to rate the candidate on a 1–10 scale. The rating itself is interesting. Does the reference give the person a 10 or settle on something lower, such as a 6? Remember, a 6 is really a 2. Additionally, how does the rating compare to what the candidate said in the screening interview? Wide discrepancies are alarming. In the end, you are looking for people who consistently get ratings of 8, 9, and 10 across your reference calls. Anything lower than that is a warning flag and should be examined more closely. One 6 need not be a deal breaker if other interviewers offer higher scores. Just take the time to understand why a discrepancy exists.

The last question allows you to use the information from the TORC (threat of reference check) section of the Who Interview. Test something the candidate told you by framing it as a question for the reference. For example, "The person mentioned that *you might say* he was disorganized. Can you tell me more about that?"

Again, the phrasing is important. "You might say" suggests to the reference that she has permission to talk about the subject because the candidate raised it. You might hear something like, "Wow, he told you that? Now that you mention it, he *was* disorganized. He never could keep his priorities straight. I remember this one time . . ." The Who Interview necessarily is confined to one side of the equation. Here comes the rest of the story.

We once helped a board decide whether to hire a CEO candidate. The CEO admitted during his interview process that "You may hear grumbling from my past team about my unwillingness to share information. But we were a public company, so I could not share everything with everybody."

In a reference interview with a past subordinate, we primed the pump and said, "The CEO mentioned that subordinates may grumble about his unwillingness to share information. Can you tell me more about that?"

The subordinate said, "Did he say that? That's not it. It's that the liar would never share any negative feedback to your face, but once you walked out of the room, he'd stab you in the back six ways to Sunday! He did that to everybody, and it really killed our trust in him. Three of our best people left over it."

Bingo! There's the gold at the end of the rainbow. That is why you do reference interviews. Who would want to hire somebody who lies and scares off great performers?

Avoid accepting a candidate's reference list at face value

Jay Jordan of the Jordan Company offered this advice based on his experience with hiring CEOs. "The best way to learn about a CEO is not to talk to their bosses, but to their subordinates. You want to get down two or three levels—to the district sales managers, say—and learn how the person interacts. You are going to get more honest answers. If you want to find out about a football team, the last person you talk to is the head coach. Don't believe the coach. You talk to the players and the trainer and the managers."

References from your own network offer yet another avenue for gathering objective, unbiased data. Investment professionals use this tactic extensively, and busy executives are beginning to put it into practice where they can. John Zillmer of Allied Waste is one of them. "I'm a real believer in reference interviews from people that you know, not just people given by the candidate." Note, however, that labor laws in some countries, such as Canada, do not allow for this type of reference checking without first getting permission from the candidate.

When Jim Crown of Bank One's search committee was evaluating Jamie Dimon for the CEO slot, he turned extensively to his own network.

"He had recently been fired by Sandy Weill at Citibank. I had worked at Salomon Brothers, which was owned by Citibank. There were people who were still there who'd worked with Jamie, so I had people I had known a long time to call. I knew people who knew Jamie and who knew Sandy Weill, so I was able to learn more about the situation.

"We talked with bosses and subordinates and peers. You hear some things that concern you—that Jamie was so driven that he could be hard on people. He did not suffer fools gladly. He was clearly capable of some impolitic decisions, based on the fight he had with Sandy, which was well publicized.

"What came out, but only after a number of interviews, was his strong sense of doing what is right and his objectivity. The organization we had was rife with politics and political intrigue. It was pretty clear that Jamie had no patience for any of that, which was exactly what we wanted."

As we wrote in a previous chapter, this is a case where the selection committee did its job to near perfection, in part because it reached out to informal "references" who had been out on the front lines. Try to do the same.

Hearing or understanding the code for risky candidates

In all likelihood your biggest problem won't be getting people to speak with you. The tactics we have described should remove most of the lingering barriers you face. But speaking and hearing are two different skills. Nearly half the industry leaders we interviewed warned that you can still get poor information from a reference call if you fail to read between the lines.

Jim Gordon of the Edgewater Funds has experienced this firsthand. "I have actually found instances where we have called people for references and have gotten excellent recommendations. Then I call someone I know very closely who knows and has worked with the person, and I've gotten a totally different and negative reference."

Why such false positives? The culprit is basic human behavior. People don't like to give a negative reference. They want to help their former colleagues, not hurt them. They want to avoid conflict, not walk right into it. Just as important, they want to feel good about themselves. As Robert Hurst told us, "People don't want to nail somebody in references."

John Sharpe from Four Seasons Hotels and Resorts agreed. "Nobody will come back to you to say that somebody is awful. But if they just confirm dates of employment, that is a bad sign. If somebody really thinks that a person is good, they're going to do more than that."

Your best defense is to pay very close attention to *what* people say and *how* they say it. Knowingly or not, most people speak in a kind of common code when they want to indicate that a candidate is problematic. The code is often not hard to break, but you have to keep your ears open. Under the pressure of a hiring decision, even obvious clues can slide right past otherwise highly astute people.

Stacy Schusterman, CEO of Samson Investment Company, told us a story of a key hire she made where she didn't hear the code. "I was doing a CFO hiring process and talking with a reference who said, 'If you are willing to have a guy disagree with you, then hire this person.' I realized afterward that the reference was trying to tell me that the person is a bull in a china shop. And the person turned out to be a bull. I should have listened harder or asked more follow-up questions."

You can be fairly certain references are speaking in code when they qualify a response with the same "if . . . then" formulation that fooled Stacy Schusterman. When you hear that, pull out your decoder ring and get curious about what's really being said.

Um's and *er*'s are another code for unspoken problems. Robert Hurst described this as "the reference who hesitates with the tough question." When you ask, "How did so-and-so do?" you want to hear tremendous enthusiasm, not *um*'s and *er*'s and carefully chosen words. A reference who hesitates is typically trying hard not to say something that will condemn your candidate or put him- or herself at legal risk. Time for your decoder ring again. What is the reference *not* saying? There might, in fact, be a good reason for the hesitation—work relationships are complicated—but until you ask, you'll never know.

Lukewarm or qualified praise also is likely to signal ambivalence or worse about a candidate. As Jeff Aronson, a managing principal at Centerbridge Partners, put it, "Faint praise in reference interviews is damning praise." We agree. The absence of enthusiasm is a terrible sign. You don't have a positive reference just because everything sounds good. Neutral, ho-hum references full of faint praise are code for bad references.

A truly positive reference, by contrast, should brim with tremendous enthusiasm and obvious admiration. It will lack hesitation and hedging. The reference's belief in the former colleague will come through in how he or she talks about the person. That excitement and spark are the clearest indicators that you are both talking about the same A Player.

DECIDE WHO TO HIRE

THE SKILL-WILL BULL'S-EYE

The goal of the "Select" step of the <u>A</u> Method is to gather the facts you need to decide if somebody's skill (what they *can* do) and will (what they *want* to do) match your scorecard. This is a person's skill-will profile. When a candidate's skill-will profile matches up perfectly with the requirements outlined on your scorecard, your candidate hits the skill-will bull's-eye.

You will have plenty of data at this point to rate your score-

C Player

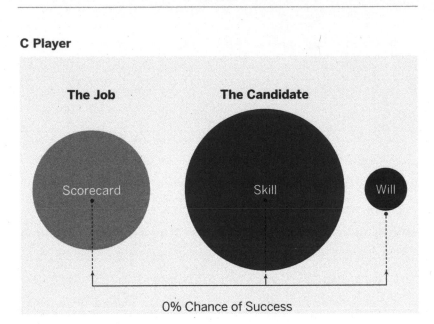

The Job — The Candidate

Scorecard · Skill · Will

0% Chance of Success

card with a high degree of accuracy. Your goal after the Who and focused interviews is to decide whether or not to continue the process with a particular candidate.

Begin by examining skill. Skill has to do with a candidate's ability to achieve the individual outcomes on your scorecard. When you believe there is a 90 percent or better chance the candidate can achieve an outcome based on the data you gathered during the interview, rate him or her an A for that outcome. When the data does not support that conclusion, give the candidate a lower rating for that outcome, such as a B or C. Repeat this process for each outcome.

Next, evaluate will. Will has to do with the motivations and competencies a candidate brings to the table. For each competency, ask yourself the same question as before. Does

A Player

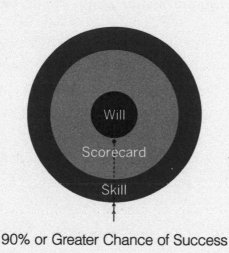

90% or Greater Chance of Success

the data suggest there is a 90 percent or better chance that the candidate will display that competency? If so, rate him or her an A for that particular competency. Otherwise, give the candidate a B or C. Repeat the process for each competency.

An A Player is someone whose skill *and* will match your scorecard. Anything less is a B or C, no matter the experience or seeming talent level.

How will you know when you have hit the skill-will bull's-eye? When (1) you are 90 percent or more confident that a candidate can get the job done because his or her skills match the outcomes on you scorecard, and (2) you are 90 percent or more confident that the candidate will be a good fit because his or her will matches the mission and competencies of the role.

DECIDE Who to Hire

RED FLAGS: WHEN TO DIVE BENEATH THE SURFACE

Some behavioral clues emerge during the hiring process that can indicate potential risks. Think of these as red flags. The flags themselves are not the deal killers, but they are likely to signal that there is something worth exploring beneath the surface.

Based on our experience, the major flags during the hiring process include:

- Candidate does not mention past failures.
- Candidate exaggerates his or her answers.
- Candidate takes credit for the work of others.
- Candidate speaks poorly of past bosses.
- Candidate cannot explain job moves.
- People most important to candidate are unsupportive of change.
- For managerial hires, candidate has never had to hire or fire anybody.
- Candidate seems more interested in compensation and benefits than in the job itself.
- Candidate tries too hard to look like an expert.
- Candidate is self-absorbed.

While none of these red flags in itself is sufficient for a thumbs-down, they do tend to correlate highly with people who, while they appear to be A Players, sink down to the B and C level once a hire is made. That's why you need to take a hard look at the data when you see too many red flags. Decision time is coming. You don't want to go all this way only to get it wrong at the end.

MARSHALL GOLDSMITH'S BEHAVIORAL WARNING SIGNS

Nobody has studied behavioral warning signs more than Marshall Goldsmith, named by *BusinessWeek* as one of the most influential practitioners of leadership development in history. In his bestseller *What Got You Here Won't Get You There,* Goldsmith identifies twenty behavioral derailers that can hurt an executive's career. When we asked him which of those derailers to consider during the hiring process, he offered this list.

"*Winning too much*. I would look out for people in the hiring process who boast about winning battles that do not matter that much. For example, a friend of mine was boasting about how he bought a toy and then found somebody else across town who was selling it for half the price. So he told me about how he returned it, drove across town, and bought the cheaper one. He won all right. But he spent two hours of his time to save $10. So his need to win in that way makes him do stupid things. You should beware of candidates who need to win to an unhealthy extent because they will be battling you and your colleagues over petty things.

"*Adding too much value* is easy to look for. If you are talking and you throw out an idea, does the candidate try to add too many of his own ideas to yours? If so, it implies that your idea was not sufficiently good on its own. It is a small indicator of ego gone awry.

"*Starting a sentence with 'no,' 'but,' or 'however'* during the interview process. 'Yes, that is a great idea' is the right answer. 'No, I agree with you but' is the symptom of somebody with an overactive ego who might be challenging to work with.

"*Telling the world how smart we are.* The unhealthy display is taking excessive credit, especially for a leadership role. For the leader, being all about me is bad.

"*Making destructive comments* about previous colleagues is a huge red flag. Because once this person works for you, he or she will make the same needless sarcastic comments about you!

"*Passing the buck.* Blaming is always bad. Winners don't blame.

"*Making excuses.* Ask people what their challenges were. If they say that their biggest challenges were not their fault but other people's fault, that shows they do not take responsibility for their performance.

"*The excessive need to 'be me.'* Listen for comments like 'That's just me, I'm not organized.' 'That's just me, I'm impatient.' 'That's just me, I don't include other people in decisions. That's just the way I am.' Beware. Somebody who has an excessive need to 'be me' is telling you that they are not open to adapt their style to fit your culture or your company and should not be hired."

DECIDE *WHO* TO HIRE

You've reached the moment of truth! You have built a score-card, sourced candidates, conducted four types of interviews on each candidate, and collected mountains of data. Now it is time to make your selection. Of these candidates, who should you hire?

With all of this great data, the decision should be easy. Here is what you do:

1. Take out your scorecards that you have completed on each candidate.

2. Make sure you have rated all of the candidates on the scorecard. If you have not given each candidate an overall A, B, or C grade, do so now. Make any updates you need to based on the reference interviews. Look at the data, consider the opinions and observations of the interview team, and give a final grade.

3. If you have no A's, then restart your process at the second step: source.

4. If you have one A, decide to hire that person.

5. If you have multiple A's, then rank them and decide to hire the best A from among them.

Congratulations! You have decided who you should hire. And if you followed the <u>A</u> Method carefully, the chances are good that this person will delight you.

But wait, you are not finished. Have you heard the riddle about the five frogs on a log? It goes like this: Five frogs are on a log and one decides to jump off. How many are left? If you answered "five," you are correct. Deciding to do something and actually doing it are two different things.

You have decided who you should hire.

Now it is time to take the final step: selling the person on actually joining your team.

HOW TO SELECT AN A PLAYER

1. **SCREENING INTERVIEW:** Conduct a twenty- to thirty-minute screening interview, using the four key questions. Probe for more information by using the "What? How? Tell me more" framework. Filter out obvious B and C Players from your hiring pipeline.

2. **WHO INTERVIEW:** Conduct a Who Interview of one and a half to three hours by walking chronologically through a candidate's career, using the same five questions for each job or chapter in the person's work history. The hiring manager and one other colleague should conduct the interview in tandem.

3. **FOCUSED INVERVIEW(S):** Involve others in the hiring process by assigning team members to conduct interviews that focus on the outcomes and/or competencies on the scorecard.

4. **CANDIDATE DISCUSSION:** Following each day of interviews, grade the scorecard using the skill-will framework. Advance those whose skill (what they are fundamentally good at doing) and will (what they want to do, and in what type of culture) match the mission, outcomes, and competencies on your scorecard. Look for people whom you would rate an A on the critical outcomes and key competencies. Nobody is perfect, but seek those who are strong in the most important places of your scorecard.

5. **REFERENCE INTERVIEW:** Conduct seven reference calls with people you choose from the Who Interview. Ask the candidate to set up the calls to break through the gatekeepers while minimizing your own effort.

6. **FINAL DECISION:** Repeat your analysis of the skill-will profile to ensure you still have a bull's-eye.

FIVE

SELL

The Top Five Ways to Seal the Deal

Most managers fail to sell a candidate.

Imagine putting all of that work into finding Mr. or Ms. Right and then losing them in the eleventh hour! Imagine the frustration, the embarrassment, the anxiety. Don't fumble the ball as you run across the goal line. You are not finished until your candidate becomes an employee.

In this chapter, you will learn the five ways to seal the deal with confidence. Sell is the fourth and final step in the <u>A</u> Method for Hiring.

The key to successfully selling your candidate to join your company is putting yourself in his or her shoes. Care about what they care about. It turns out that candidates tend to care about five things, so make sure that you address each of these five areas until you get the person to sign on the dotted line. The five areas, which we call the five F's of selling, are: fit, family, freedom, fortune, and fun.

- *Fit* ties together the company's vision, needs, and culture with the candidate's goals, strengths, and values. "Here is where we are going as a company. Here is how you fit in."
- *Family* takes into account the broader trauma of changing jobs. "What can we do to make this change as easy as possible for your family?"
- *Freedom* is the autonomy the candidate will have to make his or her own decisions. "I will give you ample freedom to make decisions, and I will not micromanage you."
- *Fortune* reflects the stability of your company and the overall financial upside. "If you accomplish your objectives, you will likely make [*compensation amount*] over the next five years."
- *Fun* describes the work environment and personal relationships the candidate will make. "We like to have a lot of fun around here. I think you will find this is a culture you will really enjoy."

SELLING FIT

Fit is by far the most important point to sell. Just as you are looking for a person who can be an A Player in a role, so the best candidates are looking for roles where they can be A Players. The better the fit, the higher the likelihood of success. Selling fit helps A Players see what you have already learned by going through the A Method.

Fit means showing the candidate how his or her goals, talents, and values fit into your vision, strategy, and culture. People want to make an impact in the world. They want to be needed. They want to be part of something that feels right. Selling fit means showing a candidate how all of these needs will be met when he or she works with you.

Alec Gores uses this approach with every hire. "I tell them the vision and where we are heading, and they get excited," he said. "They have to understand my vision. They have to become part of the formula. We are all in the same boat. We make money the same way, and we go forward the same way. I don't just hire people and say, 'This is the position.' We are going to succeed as a team and make money together."

Mark Stone is a senior managing director of the Gores Group. His advice put it about as clearly and succinctly as possible: "Show that you are as concerned with the fit for them as you are in the fit for you. Ninety-nine percent of your competitors are not doing that. It is a key differentiator. You will be the one who cares enough to see if there is something for *them* here. Everybody else is concerned with just finding out if there is a match for *us* here."

Gabriel Echavarría, chairman and director Consejo Corporativo of the Corona S.A. Organization, a ceramics company based in Colombia, focuses of necessity on the cultural aspects of fit.

Corona knows going in that the people it wants to hire are good fits for the positions available. The company's rigorous interview and assessment process gives it a clear window into the goals, strengths, and values of its recruits. The challenge, Echavarría told us, is to walk them through the larger fit with company and culture.

"The first thing you have to do is talk to them about the company. You have to sell the company and the vision of the company and the potential of the company. Nobody who is worth anything is going to go into a company where they don't see real potential with the company and a strong fit with their goals and abilities. The most valuable commodity they have is their time. If they are truly an A Player, they are going to value the potential of the company."

Next, Echavarría brings candidates to Corona and lets them walk around and meet the people there to understand their culture. "Our corporate culture is low-key. It is a family company, not a public company. We have a high appreciation for values. We don't like people who are too ostentatious or too self-sufficient. We are multinational, so we need people who can adapt to foreign cultures and our company culture."

Not until all three elements—position, company, and culture—are aligned does Echavarría assume he has a fit.

SELLING FAMILY

Gabriel Echavarría also makes heavy use of the second F in the five F's of selling: family. He uses family ties as a lure to recruit A Players.

"Foreign nationals who have spouses from Colombia are great targets," he said. "These are people with degrees from

Harvard, Northwestern, Cornell, and Stanford—very high-level people. We can recruit them to Colombia because spouses want the kids to grow up in this country, especially the mothers."

More than any American leader we interviewed, Echavarría makes a point of personally welcoming the spouses and children of candidates.

"We have a whole part of our process that is dedicated to showing the families around, sightseeing, and having dinners—really making them feel at home. That's one way we are able to sell the best candidates on making not only a career shift but a lifestyle shift to come to Colombia."

For Echavarría, families pose an opportunity to recruit people. Sometimes, though, families pose the biggest obstacle for successfully hiring an A Player. Spouses and children quite reasonably resist job changes that threaten to turn their lives upside down, separating them from friends, changing schools, and forcing them to start from scratch.

Take the situation John Malone, the chairman of Liberty Media, faced. He wanted Greg Maffei to join his team as CEO of Liberty Media. Maffei was blue-chip all the way—formerly the CFO of both Microsoft and Oracle as well as a Harvard MBA—but his family had put down roots in Seattle and had no desire to leave.

"The hardest part was to get Greg to move from Seattle to Denver," Malone said. "He has four kids. His wife was very active in local philanthropy. They were totally tied into the Seattle community. Really, the challenge was to get him and his family sufficiently excited to get them to move down here. I was not going to have a commuting CEO."

How did he do it? "It's all about the relationship," Malone said. "During nearly every conversation I had with Greg, I asked, 'How is your wife feeling about this? How excited are your kids to live in Denver?' "

In every conversation with Maffei, Malone emphasized the benefits of living in Denver, including the easy access to the mountains for skiing or hiking. Ultimately, the message got through, and Maffei and his family made the move.

Sometimes sealing the deal takes more than asking about a would-be hire's family. Sometimes you have to show the love in no uncertain terms. The best example that we know of originated with the executive assistant to the CEO of one of our clients located in Austin, Texas.

The person they were wooing was interviewing for the role of head of sales for North America. He was from "up north"—a Yankee. And although this Yankee wanted the job, his family did not want the move. So the assistant, whose magnificent name is Tex Chance, put together a care package the size of Texas. She hired a videographer to shoot footage of happy families water-skiing on Lake Travis. She included a real-estate summary report of the ten best listings in Austin, according to the family's tastes. And then, just to ice the cake, she stuffed two cowboy boots full of tequila and tickets to some of Austin's great live music performances for the couple to enjoy. In the end, the spouse and her kids were sold, the candidate accepted the job, and the whole family moved lock, stock, and barrel to the Lone Star State.

Give John Malone and Tex Chance gold stars for persistence, but these stories don't always work out so well. Time and again, we have seen A Players from managers to CEOs showered with gifts and attention only to drop out of the process at the eleventh hour because their families were not on board.

Kelvin Thompson of Heidrick & Struggles described his own efforts to wrestle with this predicament. "I said to an associate the other day that we change people's lives. We change the life of the executive we are putting in. And we change their families and the employees. In the United States, it is expected in some bizarre way that the family follows. You go outside the United States and that isn't the case. Understanding the social and family environment an executive lives in is key to their agreeing to accept a position. If you fail to understand that, you will have an executive who drops out at the last stage of the search process."

So important is the family in the decision-making process that Greg Alexander, the CEO of Sales Benchmark Index, advocates concentrating your attention there in this last stage, not on the candidate him- or herself.

"When hiring for small companies, the person who needs to be sold is never the candidate. The candidate would not be there if he were not sold. Focus on selling the spouse, children, parents, and friends of the candidate. They will have a much greater role in the decision for these types of situations. The candidate will look to them for the tough call. Better have them in your camp, or you won't get the candidate."

A word of caution as you contemplate all this: be sincere. The five F's aren't tools for manipulating people. They are areas on which you will want to focus deep and honest attention now that you have come to the end of the recruiting process.

Lee Pillsbury, chairman and CEO of Thayer Lodging Group, a privately held real-estate operating company, sets a good example for how to think about the families of your employees, not just when you are trying to seal the deal but after you bring them on board.

"I have a commitment to their families and their kids. As their kids mature, I make it a priority to personally get to know each of their kids, to advise and counsel them, and to take an interest in their success—to help them get summer jobs, complete a college application, deal with all those types of things. You need to be committed to the success of the people who are working around you in all their domains."

As all these stories suggest, once you are sold on a candidate, you have to sell him or her—and all the people who come along with him or her, from kids to parents—on you. So bring them to town and show them around. Hire a real-estate broker to give them a tour of possible neighborhoods and schools. Take them to dinner. Introduce them to the other awesome families of your teammates. And when the kids are in bed, drink some tequila together.

SELLING FREEDOM

A Players have never liked being micromanaged. It runs against their grain—the inherent characteristics that make them standouts in the first place. That's even more true of Gen-X and Gen-Y A Players. Nothing will scare them off faster than the prospect of working for an overly directive boss or board. They're looking for positions where they will be left alone to excel.

The problem is that offering the sort of freedom A Players demand and expect scares some executives because it makes them feel like they are giving up control. This is one of the great paradoxes of management. In reality, great leaders gain more control by ceding control to their A Players. They know they are bringing talented people onto their team. The scorecard tells them that, and the scorecard also tells new hires the outcomes by which they will be measured. Once it's all out on the table like that, there is no need for micromanagement. Instead, you need to create an environment where A Players like these can thrive.

George Buckley of 3M grants freedom by building trust with his employees. "A lot of CEOs think the role of the CEO is to be aloof, like a judge in a courtroom," he told us. "But the role of the CEO is to inspire people, and you cannot inspire people unless you get to know them and them you. Don't cut corners on that. It takes energy. CEOs are sometimes afraid to be real people. If you want to extract as much value as possible out of somebody in an organization, you have to let them be themselves.

"Maybe they talk too much. Maybe they are awkward in front of others. Nobody is perfect. It is not about immediate competency; it's about confidence that builds that competency. If you know that I am confident in you, you are likely to take more risks, to work a little harder, because you know that I am not going to take your head off if something doesn't work perfectly. That builds competence. Extend the hand of trust. And occasionally extend the hand of friendship."

Stacy Schusterman builds trust with her A Player candidates by encouraging them to evaluate her as a manager. "If they are going to be a senior person, they are going to want a higher degree of autonomy. I encourage the candidate to do reference checks on me so they can understand how I work with people." Nothing sells freedom more than giving candidates free access to the people around you so they can ask whatever they want about your style.

Some organizations build their entire culture around freedom. Tudor Investment Corporation is a great example of that. "We look at ourselves as a support organization for great entrepreneurs who want to work collectively with other entrepreneurs," Paul Tudor Jones said. "They have almost entire freedom over the way they run their own investment-making decision process."

In the not-for-profit sector, a sense of purpose and the freedom to pursue it are often the best selling points a manager has to work with. George Hamilton, head of the Institute for Sustainable Communities, says that the new hires he pursues know the hours will be long and the pay poor, but they are still A Players and have to be approached as such.

"We try to convince them that what we are doing makes a big difference in people's lives, and it does. We do tremendous work in the field. But we're also very business-like, very results-oriented, and that's extremely appealing to a lot of people.

"They need to feel they will be productive. They want to

know what their responsibilities are going to be and if they will have enough opportunities to show what they can do. Managing these people can be a real challenge because you have to create enough space for them to show what they can do."

Freedom matters to today's workforce, and especially to the most valuable among them. A Players want to operate without micromanagement, develop their own leadership styles, and prove their own worth. Show them that both you personally and your organizational culture will support their need for freedom, and you'll go a long way toward sealing the deal.

SELLING FORTUNE

If nothing else seems to be working, you can always throw money at a hire you are trying to land, right? Actually, wrong.

Research shows that while money can be a disincentive if it is too low or not linked to performance, it rarely is the key motivator.* A raise given today is usually forgotten by tomorrow. As Honeywell Aerospace CEO Robert Gillette told us, "If all you have to sell is the compensation, that is not good." To be sure, money is one piece of the package, but it never stands alone.

That doesn't mean you can ignore it. Compensation will enter the equation eventually, and you can take advantage of

---

* "One More Time: How Do You Motivate Employees?" Frederick Herzberg, *Harvard Business Review,* January–February 1968.

that fact by demonstrating how a candidate would be rewarded if he or she joined your company. Carl Lindner, the chairman and founder of American Financial Group in Cincinnati, has made good use of this strategy. He said, "I believe in encouraging people to look at our record earnings, growth, and market value. I often share with candidates the personal success those working with us have obtained in terms of compensation and personal wealth."

The pay level you end up discussing inevitably is dictated by both the external and internal markets. Candidates will benchmark themselves against their current compensation and what they believe they can command in the external market. Managers, in turn, will try to apply internal compensation guidelines, which may or may not have been benchmarked against external sources.

Allstate chairman Ed Liddy captured this practical reality when he said, "There is no such thing as a bargain in the labor market. It is easy to underpay or overpay. You can't try to steal them because they will want to go somewhere else. And you can't throw too much money at them because other people will find out and that will make them mad."

Liddy's advice, like so many others we spoke to, was to "pay people on a performance basis." He added, "We have used it here at Allstate very successfully. That gets you good people, people who believe in themselves."

We endorse this strategy while also recommending that you link variable compensation to an employee's performance against the scorecard. Scorecards define A performance and provide objective metrics for monitoring it. Linking bonuses to scorecard attainment ensures you pay top compensation only when you get A performance.

Gabriel Echavarría of Corona has done exactly that. "Our people know every quarter where their bonuses are. Bonuses are tied to mathematical goals with eight other goals that are easily identifiable. We have had people join our company for a lower salary because they believe in the growth."

By selling fortune in the context of fit with the company's growth potential, Echavarría has been able to attract A Players who are in it for the long haul. "People join us not for six months, but for six years or ten years or thirty years."

SELLING FUN

We spend more than a third of our time, and probably better than half our waking time, at work. We might as well have fun while we are doing it.

What "fun" means, of course, is closely tied to corporate culture. We've visited start-ups where you are tempted to think you've walked into a rec center. We've also been in venerable financial institutions where fun might mean wearing a two-piece suit instead of a three-piece one.

At ghSMART, ours is a culture where another of the F's—freedom—reigns, so for us, fun means doing what you love. Geoff enjoys thinking big, developing business, and recruiting more than anything else he does. The 80 percent of his time he spends on these pursuits is pure enjoyment.

Randy launched the ghSMART Executive Learning business because he has a passion for helping people learn skills that make them more productive at work and in life. Simultaneously, he has minimized the parts of his job that make work seem more like, well, work.

On top of that, we both thoroughly enjoy every member of our team. All of us at ghSMART chose them carefully to make sure they will fit with us in every way, including our understanding of fun. Frankly, this is one of the chief selling points for people who are looking to join our company. We strive to have fun at work every single day. Once a year, too, we hold a company summit at a nice location such as Napa Valley or Hilton Head, and invite our employees' spouses to join us.

We are not alone. When John Zillmer told us how he decided to join Allied Waste as CEO, he hit on almost all of the five F's, but the one he punctuated his thoughts with was the last F: fun.

"The board made an attractive offer—it was not extraordinary by any means. It was a chance to join a company that Ed Evans, my SVP of HR, calls a $6 billion start-up that needed some direction. Perfect! That is the kind of place I love. They needed somebody who had seen this done before. I felt that my experiences would be a very good fit with the state of evolution. I did not have to go back to work again. What really mattered was that I felt I could make a difference and that it could be fun."

What's fun, of course, varies from person to person. In John Zillmer's case, fun was the chance to use his talents and experience to maximum advantage. Clearly, by those standards, he has been having a blast.

FIVE WAVES OF SELLING

Selling a would-be hire is a matter of understanding which of the five F's really matter to a candidate and focusing attention on those levers to overcome a candidate's concerns. But when do you sell?

We have presented this "Sell" chapter as the last step in the <u>A</u> Method. In reality, selling is something you should be doing throughout the entire process. Like sourcing, selling requires constant attention.

Over the years, we have identified five distinct phases of the hiring process that merit increased selling effort on your part. Think of these as waves to overcome. If you don't increase your sales energy, you won't get your candidate over the crest of the wave to the next phase. The waves are:

1. When you source
2. When you interview
3. The time between your offer and the candidate's acceptance
4. The time between the candidate's acceptance and his or her first day
5. The new hire's first one hundred days on the job

The emphasis on interest and talents during the sourcing process provides the first opportunity for you to gauge which of the five F's are going to matter to the candidate. Mark Stone put it well when he said, "You sell from the moment you start the whole hiring process. It all starts with understanding where somebody is with their interests. It helps you spot where their hooks are, but to spot the hooks, you have to listen. 'Where are you today? What is it you are really seeking?' "

A second reason to sell from the outset, Stone told us, "is that people will let down their guard earlier. You get a faster and richer view of who they are and what they want. Then you can sell this as clearly the right next move for them."

Selling during the interview process typically happens toward the end of each interview. As we wrote earlier, we recommend you set up each session by saying something like this: "We'd like to spend the first part of this interview getting to know you. Then we'd like to give you the opportunity to get to know us."

The question time at the end is when you put on your sales hat, assuming you still see potential in the candidate. By paying attention to what the candidate says during the interview, you'll have a clearer idea how to frame the offer that ultimately will attract that person to your company.

Let's say, for example, you're interviewing a candidate for a curator's job at an art museum, and at the end, she asks whether the museum fully funds continuing education for its employees. Now you know two things: (1) she is interested in improving her weak spots and enhancing her expertise, and (2) the more attractive your continuing education opportunities— not just degree programs, say, but travel as well—the better the likelihood she will say yes if you ultimately decide to extend an offer. If that is the case, then sell that point.

The third opportunity to sell falls between your offer and their acceptance. Too often, managers back away at this point, on the mistaken notion that prospective hires "need time to think about it." They might well need time, but this is likely to have been a prolonged courtship. Backing too far away at this point can feel a lot like a cold shoulder, as George Buckley found out when the board of directors recruited him to become the CEO of 3M.

"The board was fastidious in its scrutiny of candidates," Buckley said. "I would score the board 95 percent in this particular examination. Why not 100 percent? They got the fish on the line, but getting it in the net was one of the challenges. After some unproductive negotiations, I was inclined to decline the position. The problem was with the intermediate lawyers who were negotiating on behalf of 3M. They cared little for me as a person or for 3M as a company and it nearly backfired. I told the board that I felt like a nonperson in these discussions. It was like they were buying a refrigerator, not a person. They had not made the human connection."

Luckily, the chairman of the search committee intervened and pulled the negotiations out of the fire, and Buckley joined 3M anyway. Another candidate might have walked, forcing them to devote time and resources to doing the whole process over again.

Instead of putting people in the deep freeze, assume they have received an attractive counteroffer from their current employer and are considering other options at the same time. These are A Players, after all. Silence is your worst enemy at this stage.

Stay in touch with them on a regular basis. Pinpoint their concerns using the five F's as your guide. Show them how much they will fit with and contribute to the company. Woo their families. Commit to giving them freedom and autonomy to do their job. Address financial concerns. And involve them in the fun your employees are already having. Occasionally you will turn a candidate off by being too ardent a suitor, but our experience has been that managers undersell far more often than they oversell.

The goal, of course, is to try to get a candidate to say yes as quickly as you can, but don't assume that getting there is the end of the chase. Candidates still have time to get cold feet and back out. They still have counteroffers and competing offers on the table. Their families are still concerned about how the job will affect them, seeding doubt in the candidates' minds. Until they've committed 100 percent to their new lives, they will be at risk of leaving and not be as effective as they might be.

We suggest celebrating their acceptance by sending something meaningful, such as flowers, balloons, or a gift certificate. Make a splash. Continue to stay in touch. Keep listening for concerns related to the five F's and address them as soon as they come up.

Even though we knew better, ghSMART made a mistake during this wave of the sales process not long ago. We extended an offer to a candidate who excitedly accepted it. He was about to get married, so we agreed to talk after his wedding. We even sent him champagne to toast his future. We thought we would give him space, given all of the changes going on in his life, but maybe we overdid it.

A few weeks later, after the honeymoon, he told us he wasn't going to join us after all. His new bride thought it was too risky to change jobs at that pivotal point in his life. We were shocked. *They'd drunk our champagne!* But we had fallen down on our end by failing to sell his new family—his bride—during this critical juncture in his decision-making process.

Finally, the big day comes when your new A Player joins the company. But guess what? You still aren't done selling. Research shows an alarming failure rate among new hires in the first one hundred days. People get buyer's remorse during these early months and are tempted to cut their losses. You can mitigate that risk by investing in a strong on-boarding program. That entails more than just a welcome lunch and short orientation given by the HR department. You, the hiring manager or board member, have to make sure your new A Player has every opportunity to succeed.

The good news is that all the work you have done up to this point—the scorecard, sourcing, and selection process—should have given you enough insight to create a program to ensure the new hire's success.

Paul Lattanzio, senior managing director at BGCP and a longtime user of the A Method, said, "This method gives you the insights about the person that typically take you a year of working with them to figure out. That helps you get the relationship off on the right foot from day one." And getting things off on the right foot will help you retain the A Player you worked so hard to hire.

PERSISTENCE PAYS OFF

A seasoned executive once asked us what we thought was the single most important aspect to selling a candidate on joining a company. We knew from our research that there actually was a one-word answer to that question: persistence. Great leaders are persistent. They don't take the first no for an answer. They keep positive pressure on the A Players they want until they get them. From the first sourcing call to the last sales call, they never let up.

Robert Hurst told us a story that illustrates this point. "If you find somebody you want, go after them. In the case of a public insurance company we owned, we were looking for a number-two executive and not the number-one. Some of us on the board knew the number-one should go, but the number-one did not know that. We found a great hire. He said he would not take the number-two spot and wait several years to become number-one. So I would call him every couple of weeks and say, 'I think there is a chance to be number-one right away.'

"We ultimately asked the CEO to leave, and we put in the new man as the CEO right away. He would have done something else if we had not gone after him in a very aggressive way. That process went on for four to five months, and we got him. He did a great job. The company needed an A Player. And we got one, and the stock went up five times over a couple of years."

John Howard, the CEO of BSMB, told his own story about a famous deal maker who purchased a consumer products company. It is another wonderful illustration of how the persistent pursuit of A Players can pay off.

Howard began by describing how the deal maker approached a newly acquired property that was quickly going downhill—a disaster. "He knew he had to change management and tried to figure out how to get the best guy in the industry. He had identified the number-two guy in a good competitor. He romanced him by flying down to meet him one-on-one. He got personal with him. He built a relationship. He wanted him because he was someone who had grown up in the business and the deal maker knew he could turn around the business quickly. He was the man.

"But the question was how to get the guy. The deal maker has a house near where the guy lived, so every time he flew down, he would meet with him. The candidate was making, like, $175K—I don't know if that is exactly right—and the deal maker kept offering more and more and more money. He had offered more than double what the candidate was making before, but the guy was still reticent. He was a small-town guy and was intimidated by New York. While he'd never graduated from high school, he was the smartest guy I have ever met. The deal maker kept after him, and more and more the guy's wife came up as the reason for not coming on board, but it was not clear if it was real or an excuse.

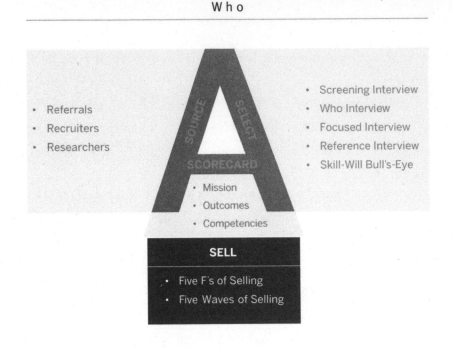

"The deal maker finally asked him to come to New York with his wife. By this time, the deal maker had offered three or four times the guy's present salary. He flies him up in his private plane. He takes them to a fancy co-op overlooking the river. He has this penthouse on top, and he took them up and said, 'This is where you would live, care of the company. This would be taken care of.' Everything was windows all around, and all you are seeing is New York. Everything is glowing. It's possible that the deal maker waited until night to make the view even better than during the day.

"Then they go downstairs, and there is a Porsche 911. He said, 'This would be your car if you came to this company.'

"Then they go out to dinner at the fanciest French restaurant the deal maker could find, which he knew they would like because he knew the CEO candidate and his wife were food-

> **HOW TO SELL A PLAYERS**
>
> 1. Identify which of the five F's really matter to the candidate: fit, family, freedom, fortune, or fun.
> 2. Create and execute a plan to address the relevant F's during the five waves of selling: during sourcing, during interviews, between offer and acceptance, between acceptance and the first day, and during the first one hundred days on the job.
> 3. Be persistent. Don't give up until you have your A Player on board.

ies. He has this big box on the table and says to the CEO candidate's wife, 'I know you are concerned about New York and how it can be cold in the winter.' He takes a chinchilla coat out of the box and says, 'You can keep this. Whatever you decide, this is my gift to you.'

"He finally got up to like $850K in salary, plus the apartment and car and coat, and the candidate accepted. Within one year, he had totally turned around the company.

"The reason I know this was because we bought the company from the deal maker a few years later and delivered him a great return. We also made a great return on our investment. We held the company for four years and made twenty times our money in that time."

The moral of the story, Howard told us, is this: "You've got to do whatever it takes when you are sure you have identified the right person. You do whatever you can." You might not be hiring at a level that justifies a penthouse apartment or a new car. But at any level, persistence pays off.

SIX

YOUR GREATEST OPPORTUNITY

The <u>A</u> Method is simple and practical. The more than four hundred CEOs, business billionaires, and other successful leaders and investors who participated in the research for this book aren't theorists. These captains of industry have spent their lifetime in the trenches, making businesses grow. They know where the biggest problems can be found and the greatest opportunities lie.

We asked these leaders what factors contributed the most to business success. They told us that "management talent" was over half the equation. The only other category to draw even 20 percent of the vote was execution. Strategy finished

What Makes a Successful Business?

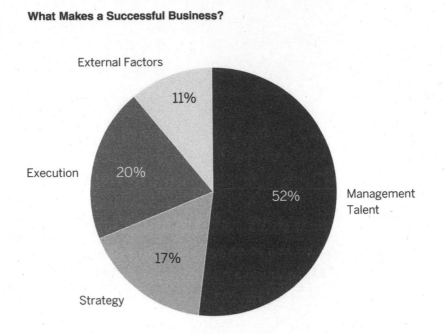

External Factors

11%

Execution

20%

52%
Management
Talent

17%

Strategy

below that, at 17 percent, and external factors—interest rates, for example—still further back at 11 percent.

Collectively, their message couldn't be clearer. Get the talent side of the equation wrong, and you will always face rough waters. You'll spend all of your time dealing with an endless torrent of *what* issues. Get it right, and you'll have clear skies, smooth seas, and easy sailing. The right *who* will take care of all of those issues.

Just ask John Varley, CEO of Barclays PLC.

"If I think about how we spend our time on the executive committee at Barclays, the biggest change since I have been named CEO is regarding people and talent," Varley told us. "It has assumed strategic proportions as far as the percentage of time it consumes. We now have a people component to the agenda weekly. And quarterly, we spend half of our off-site reviewing talent—internal development, external talent we are hiring, and so on.

"If I look at the Barclays portfolios of businesses compared to our peers', the portfolios are not that different. If you think about competitive strategy, that strategy is not that differentiated bank versus bank. So the differentiation is in execution. And execution is determined by people.

"A client in Mumbai will come to Barclays if they think our people are distinctive. Whether they are a corporate or personal customer, they want to be smart in their choice of provider. We want customers to come to Barclays because Barclays' people are among the best in the world."

HOW TO INSTALL THE <u>A</u> METHOD FOR HIRING IN YOUR COMPANY

You have to do ten things if you want to install the <u>A</u> Method for Hiring in your business:

1. *Make people a top priority.* The leaders we interviewed for this book told us they spend as much as 60 percent of their time thinking about people. By making it one of your top three priorities and communicating the urgency of addressing it, you can prevent your team from thinking it is just another flavor of the month that they can wait out.

2. *Follow the A Method yourself.* Great leaders don't tell people what to do. They lead by example. That gives them the right to expect others to follow.

3. *Build support among your executive team or peers.* Leaders gain momentum by engaging everybody on their executive team to follow the A Method. They use their personal relationships to garner support, hand out books such as this one to promote the idea, and even hold off-sites and workshops to supercharge the topic.

4. *Cast a clear vision for the organization and reinforce it through every communication with the broader team.* Try a message like "We are going to win with A Players," "We will succeed because we have an A Player in every role," or "Our people will serve our customers far better than the competition because our people are all A Players." Then back up these words with actions to show how the vision is transforming the team.

5. *Train your team on best practices.* Leaders ensure every manager on the team has the skills required to execute the A Method by helping them learn each step. A hands-on workshop demystifies the process and puts the simple tools in their hands.

6. *Remove barriers that impede success.* Leaders who want to be A Players in charge of teams full of other A Players work with HR to eliminate any policy, standard, or practice that gets in the way of successfully implementing the A Method. They remove any possibility for excuses based on an outdated approach.

7. *Implement new policies that support the change.* Leaders know that all of the communication in the world won't motivate some members of the team, so they put a few simple policies in place to provide a backstop for wayward colleagues:

- They place the following outcome on every manager's scorecard: "Achieve a hiring success rate of 90 percent or greater. Build and retain a team composed of 90 percent or more A Players by a certain date."
- They require a scorecard for every job requisition. No scorecard, no requisition. Managers who want help from the company's recruiting team need to provide a scorecard to get support.
- They require a Who Interview and rated scorecard before an offer can be made. The human resource group serves as a gatekeeper to ensure this actually happens. No Who Interview, no hire.

8. *Recognize and reward those who use the method and achieve results.* Captains of industry are always on the lookout for evidence that people are using the A Method, and they publicly recognize those who do. They also reward managers who achieve a 90 percent or better hiring success rate by linking a substantial portion of their bonus to that particular outcome. They know that bonuses pay for themselves through substantially increased productivity.

9. *Remove managers who are not on board.* Captains

151

short-circuit any potential for mutiny by removing those who refuse to build a better team using the method. Of course, they give people every opportunity to succeed before they make this decision, but they do not hesitate once it becomes clear that someone is not going to cooperate.

10. *Celebrate wins and plan for more change.* The best leaders celebrate their team's success by offering tangible rewards, such as a fancy dinner, a team event, or even a nice gift. They use the goodwill generated by this recognition to inspire more action in the next year. Never satisfied, they seek new and better ways to achieve the results they desire and go back to step one to implement those changes.

We've seen CEO after CEO go through this process and achieve amazing results. They build visibly stronger and more productive teams. Ultimately, the value of their companies rises well above market benchmarks.

In fact, that's a large part of what motivates us at ghSMART. We get to watch successful people become even more successful because they put the right teams in place. We see stock prices rise and deal values grow. We even get to see how the right teams can change an executive's life.

We rated one COO a B Player after conducting a Who Interview. To us, it was obvious that he did not know how to build a strong team around him. The COO was burned out from trying to do everything himself and frustrated because his team didn't seem to get it. As it turns out, he was the one who didn't quite get it.

Our rating included a warning that unless the COO learned to accept coaching, he was the wrong person in the job. We meant it as a wake-up call, and to his credit, he decided to take action. Using the A Method as a guide, he made changes to his team and hired or moved A Players into each role.

When we checked in with him nine months after his initial assessment to see how he was doing, we half expected to hear him complain once again about how tired he was. In fact, we were in for a big surprise.

"You know what?" he told us. "I feel great! I have a fantastic team working with me now. For the first time in my career, I don't have to be the first person to arrive in the morning and the last one out at night. I'm sleeping better. I'm working out. I'm spending time with my wife. And it's all because I have a team of A Players.

"This is the best team I have ever had. And because they are A Players, they are hiring more A Players. They are doing an amazing job. We are more productive now than we have ever been. I love my job!"

The CEO of this company has taken notice and considers his COO an A Player now, mostly because he has developed the key leadership skill of picking A Players to drive the business.

To repeat, you don't have to be the CEO to implement the A Method. You can do it in your function, department, or business unit just as easily. You can make a difference wherever you sit. Make the A Method and A Players a priority in your sphere of influence and encourage your team to follow your lead. Your group will benefit, and others will notice. The example you set will serve as a beacon for the rest of the company to follow.

LEGAL TRAPS TO AVOID

Hiring is serious business. We've tried to demystify the process for you and make it as simple as possible, but no one—not you, not us—can ignore the legalities of hiring. Many managers get themselves and their companies into big trouble by ignoring basic principles.

Please make sure you are in compliance with all relevant employment laws at the federal or central, provincial or state, and local levels, wherever in the world you are hiring. Work with your HR people and employment legal team to gain a thorough understanding of all the issues to be aware of, and stay in the green zone with respect to your hiring practices.

The ghSMART A Method for Hiring is legal and fair. The consistency of the process and focus on gathering data actually make it far more legal and fair than the ad hoc hiring practices commonly used by businesspeople. We have taught the A Method to more than thirty thousand managers in hundreds of companies across a dozen countries. We have never encountered legal problems for using this method, nor are we aware of any of our clients ever encountering legal problems for using the method advocated in this book.

To stay well within the law, we suggest you respect these four areas of caution:

1. *Relevance.* Do not reject candidates for reasons that are not relevant to the job. One tremendous benefit of the scorecard is that it will force you to define the outcomes and competencies required in a job before you start interviewing people. That explicit definition will keep you honest during your evaluation. Stick to the facts. Exclude issues or feelings that are irrelevant to the successful attainment of the scorecard.

2. *Standardization of hiring process.* Use the same process for all candidates regardless of their demographic group. Managers get into trouble when they consciously or inadvertently put different groups through different processes. A standard process ensures fairness across all groups.

3. *Use nondiscriminatory language during interviews and in written forms.* Saying "he or she" or "they" is better than assuming a role should be performed by a man or woman. Obviously, never use language that is derogatory toward anyone.

4. *Avoid asking candidates illegal questions.* Certain questions cannot be asked in an interview. In the United States, these questions include anything to do with marital status, intention to have children, whether or not candidates are pregnant, when they were born, where they were born, medical condition (unless specif-

ically relevant to the performance of the job), race or ethnicity, sexual orientation, or physical or mental handicaps (again, unless directly relevant to the performance of the job). The questions to avoid vary somewhat in other nations, so please check with your local HR and legal team to understand a specific country's laws before interviewing there. An ounce of prevention is always worth a pound of cure.

These steps make it easy to comply with the guidelines for hiring laid out by the Equal Employment Opportunity Commission (EEOC) or contained in the Americans with Disabilities Act of 1990 (ADA) in the United States. The same is true in other countries.

The bottom line is this: don't discriminate. Select people based on whether they are likely to be able to perform a job or not. Use the scorecard to define the standard, and the screening, Who, focused, and reference interviews to gather facts to hold up against that standard. Evaluate people based on the factors that matter for the position at hand, and on those factors only. This should enable you to enjoy the results of a hiring method that is fair, legal, and extraordinarily effective.

THOUGHTS ON BUILDING YOUR TEAM

We have focused primarily in these pages on finding and selecting A Players. But managers don't need just one A Player. They need to build an entire team of A Players. The team drives the business forward, not just a single person.

We have found over the years that the thought of hiring a full team of A Players can make many managers nervous. We have even had managers express their fears explicitly. "Aren't A Players the athletes who don't work well together?" they'll say. Or "Isn't there an inherent conflict because they all want to be the star? Shouldn't we staff our team with some A Players and lots of B Players to avoid that conflict?"

Let's not reenter the fog. Remember, an A Player is not an all-around athlete. An A Player is someone who accomplishes the goals on the scorecard, which only the top 10 percent of the people in the relevant labor pool could accomplish. And you get to define the scorecard. You determine what a job holder must accomplish. You set competencies and values consistent with your culture. So an A Player is someone who accomplishes the outcomes *you define* in a manner consistent with *your* culture and values.

If teamwork is a core value in your company, then a star athlete who wants the spotlight is not an A Player. We don't care how productive he or she might be. We have already cited several instances where clients fired a top performer who was achieving results at the expense of cultural norms and values, and we could cite many more. A Players get the job done while embracing the culture *because the scorecard ensures they fit the culture.*

A Players can and do work well together because each understands and is selected for a unique role in the broader context of the team. They don't get in one another's way because they are specialists who are particularly good at what they do.

Individually, they are A Players because you have taken the

time to match their unique motivations, talents, and values to their roles. Collectively, they form an A team because they know how to pull on the oars together. They propel your business forward by making unique contributions that add up to something greater than the sum of the parts alone. We believe that it is not only possible but also highly desirable to build an entire team of A Players.

RIDING THE RISING TIDE

You've probably heard the expression, "A rising tide lifts all boats." So it is with A Players. The right hire in the right position at the right time with the right cultural alignment echoes throughout an organization. Productivity, goals, desires, and enthusiasm all benefit when you bring in the exact person your division or unit or company needs. One client told us he thought his company's entire *aspiration* rose with every A Player he brought on board.

What you need to keep in mind, though, is that not every tide rises the same way. Some surge. Some creep slowly and steadily. While the A Players you bring in need to be attuned to your culture, the culture needs enough elasticity to embrace the A Players who can challenge you in areas where you need to be challenged.

Sir Terry Leahy, *Fortune* magazine's 2003 European Business Leader of the Year, started out as a shelf stocker at Tesco and rose to become its CEO. When Tesco decided to get into the clothing business four years ago, Leahy knew Tesco's culture as well as anyone, but he still pushed his team to break the mold.

"We brought in John Hoerner, who had been CEO of a large clothing company, to run that part of our business," Leahy told us. "The Tesco clothing business was large, but not as large as the company he ran as a retailer. John was a huge success. The business has tripled in size and is a lot more profitable. He put in the foundations of future growth and profitability.

"John was a business builder by nature, and we needed that. But he also pushed us. We could have hired someone more like us, more typical of Tesco, but that would have been the wrong hire. We knew we needed to get the best clothing person we could find and do all we could to support him. My team and I allowed him plenty of freedom and flexibility to operate as he saw fit.

"You have to have a culture that is supportive and gives people room and tolerates a bit of difference in personality. You have to have quite a mature senior management population. They have to be comfortable around big, challenging personalities and able to operate professionally and calmly as these people come into the organization. What happens when you do that is that you both benefit. Tesco has changed them. But they have changed Tesco as well."

Building a team of A Players means thinking long and hard about your business strategy and contemplating what roles you need to fill to execute it. You might be able to get there with a few tweaks to your existing team, or you could need to make substantive changes.

Either way, leaders don't wait to find the time to do this. They *make* the time. They are constantly on the lookout for

WHAT TYPES OF CEOS MAKE MONEY FOR INVESTORS?

Our clients often ask us, "What types of CEOs make money for investors?"

The proper answer is, It depends on the scorecard. Different situations call for different scorecards.

However, too many people have pressed us for the answer to the question to ignore it. They ask, "But are there some general qualities about CEOs that tend to predict success or failure?"

The answer is yes.

If you are a CEO, or want to become one, you may find this bonus section enlightening. We conducted the largest study ever done, pairing in-depth assessments of CEO traits with financial performance. What we found may make your head spin. It flies in the face of conventional wisdom.

To learn whether there is indeed a profile that can predict CEO success, we teamed up with Steve Kaplan, professor of entrepreneurship and finance at the University of Chicago, and his collaborators, professor Morten Sorensen and research assistant Mark Klebanov. Together, we analyzed the data from 313 Who Interviews we conducted on private-equity-backed CEOs from 2000 to 2005. Then we matched the CEO assessments with the actual financial performance they delivered, which we tracked down with permission from our clients.

The results were compelling and controversial. In fact, *The Wall Street Journal* ran a half-page article about this on November 19, 2007, that attracted a lot of attention.

Boards and investors have a tendency to invest in CEOs who demonstrate openness to feedback, possess great listening skills, and treat people with respect. These are executives who have mastered the soft skills. We call them "Lambs" because these CEOs tend to graze in circles, feeding on the feedback and direction of others.

Boards love Lambs because they are so easy to work with, and in fact, in our study Lambs were successful 57 percent of the time. That is not a bad success rate. A batter who hit .570 over a career could walk backward into the Hall of Fame.

The second dominant profile that emerged from our analysis was of CEOs who move quickly, act aggressively, work hard, demonstrate persistence, and set high standards and hold people accountable to them. We call these CEOs "Cheetahs" because they are fast and focused.

Cheetahs in our study were successful 100 percent of the time. This is not a rounding error. *Every single one of them* created significant value for their investors.

Conventional wisdom holds that the sort of emotional intelligence Lambs show is *the* critically important leadership quality. In fact, our analysis argues otherwise. Emotional intelligence is important, *but only when matched with the propensity to get things done.* Too many executives have fallen into the trap of accentuating their Lamb skills at the expense of their Cheetah qualities. They work hard to stay in tune with their employees. They're well liked on the shop floor and in the boardroom. There's only one problem: they don't produce value at anywhere near the rate Cheetahs do.

This isn't to say that Cheetahs lack soft skills. To the contrary, they are talented people whose soft skills played a critical role in their ascent to the top job. The difference, though, is that Cheetahs know when it is time to stop asking for feedback and to attack a target to achieve key outcomes that move a company forward.

The characteristics that make up a Cheetah or a Lamb were statistically significant predictors of success in the job. Steve Kaplan and his team have presented these findings at the University of Chicago, Harvard, Wharton, and Kellogg. We know the results hold true in private equity,

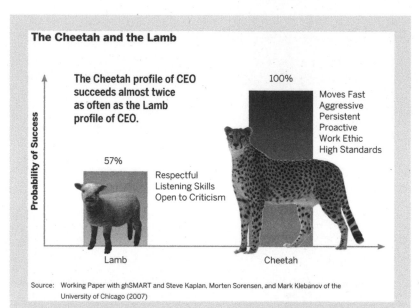

The Cheetah and the Lamb

The Cheetah profile of CEO succeeds almost twice as often as the Lamb profile of CEO.

Probability of Success

100%

Moves Fast
Aggressive
Persistent
Proactive
Work Ethic
High Standards

57%

Respectful
Listening Skills
Open to Criticism

Lamb

Cheetah

Source: Working Paper with ghSMART and Steve Kaplan, Morten Sorensen, and Mark Klebanov of the University of Chicago (2007)

and plan to study how extensible these findings are to public-company CEOs. In the meantime, you might consider how these findings apply to you.

Selim Bassoul, the CEO of Middleby Corporation, a manufacturer of restaurant cooking equipment, is a terrific example of a Cheetah. Five years ago, when Bassoul ascended to the CEO position, shareholders considered his fast-moving, bold, and persistent style a risk. However, he soon became known as a very successful CEO.

Bassoul quickly killed unprofitable product lines. With equal speed, he evaluated his team and promoted or hired similar-minded, hard-charging leaders while simultaneously reducing management layers from seven to three. To better understand customer issues, he had all unanswered customer calls forwarded to his personal cell phone. Because the company's clients are restaurants, his phone rang constantly on the weekend, peak days for restaurants. That led him to change the workweek from the standard Monday through Friday to Wednesday through Sunday. People said he couldn't do that, but he did it anyway.

Was anyone hurt by Selim Bassoul's hard-charging style? Sure, non-performers had to adjust or get out of the way. But Bassoul watched out for the people who stayed. For example, he learned from surveys that his employees wanted cleaner bathrooms. "Now," he told us, "our bathrooms are just as clean as any bathroom you have ever been in!"

Investors were never ambivalent about Bassoul once they saw his results. They saw their stake in Middleby soar by a staggering 3,500 percent over half a decade. As he explained, "We grew the stock price from $4 to $142 over the last five years. It has been fabulous growth!"

Should you always want to be a Cheetah, or do you always want to hire a Cheetah? No. But if you have the choice to be or hire somebody who errs on the side of being too fast and focused versus being slow and extremely collaborative, we recommend going with the fast and focused option. In this fast-paced age of business in which we all exist, it appears that speed and focus really count when it comes to delivering great financial results.

talented people and deploy the A Method to bring them onto their teams. They recognize that it is the most important thing they can do to ensure their long-term success.

BEYOND HIRING

We have found that most managers fall back on voodoo hiring methods when thinking about development, promotions, and succession planning. They base their actions and decisions on tenure or how well someone is performing in their current role rather than evaluating what they will need to succeed in a future role. Not surprisingly, companies misdirect billions of dollars toward futile training efforts and make promotion or succession decisions with the same failure rate as they suffer with hiring.

Retired army general Wesley Clark, one of the most decorated United States military leaders alive today, saw these dynamics over a long career that included service as the NATO supreme allied commander. When we met with General Clark, he said, "What got you promoted to one rank won't necessarily get you promoted to the next rank." The scorecard changes the higher somebody climbs in an organization, which means how you think about a person's capabilities must change. Applying the A Method, and in particular the scorecard and select portions of the method, will enable you to focus development resources on the right actions, and to promote people who will succeed in their new positions.

Ted Bililies, a ghSMART managing director, experienced this while working with both the chairman and CEO of a trillion-dollar global bank during a time of transition. The CEO realized that he had several senior executive leaders who were either not in the right roles or who had serious flaws in the functions that they were currently mandated to lead. Meanwhile, the chairman was pressuring the CEO to "know your people better," and to gather more detailed information on the suitability for promotion of his various direct reports to succeed the CEO.

Through a series of confidential and sensitive conversations with the CEO, the ghSMART team built scorecards for each role by reviewing the strategy for each business unit and its implications on each position for today and especially for two to three years out.

Next, ghSMART conducted a Who Interview with each individual business leader to learn about their success patterns and how they perceived their business unit. The team supplemented that data by interviewing twelve to twenty current and former colleagues of each executive to gain a third-party perspective, much like you would do in a reference interview.

Finally, the team presented this thorough X-ray of the top talent to the CEO and ultimately the chairman. Armed with data, the CEO was able to accelerate the development of key individuals, position others for key succession roles, and move out or redeploy others. With this same data, the chairman was able to make the ultimate decision: Who should replace the retiring CEO?

The succession decision was put into effect, and the person who took the helm was hailed publicly as exactly the right person for the role. Perhaps even more meaningful to us, the CFO told Bililies privately, "Congratulations on the smoothest CEO transition in the last fifty years."

Back when he was CEO of Brunswick, George Buckley was asked at a public meeting, "Hey, George, what is your attitude about people?"

"Look, a lot of you today are supervisors," Buckley answered. "I want you to pause for a moment and think about the very best person you have working for you. Now I want you to think about the second-best person you have working for you. Now I would like you to think about where your organization would be without them. You would be terrified if you lost them. And you would love to have ten more like them. That is how I feel about the importance of hiring, promoting, and keeping the right people."

We hope you feel the same way.

YOU CAN DO IT

The A Method propels your career forward. It allows you to achieve more career, financial, and even personal success than you ever thought possible. Seeing it all come together is truly a beautiful thing.

One of the business billionaires we visited for this book was Bill Koch. An oil and gas magnate, Koch set out in 1992 to resuscitate the United States' fortunes in the America's Cup competition, the most prestigious sailing race in the world.

Koch, it turned out, knew the basics of the A Method for hiring, but he hadn't learned them from us. Credit instead goes to his MIT basketball coach from years earlier.

"My freshman year we only won one game," he recalled. "Then the school replaced the coach with someone who had won more games than anyone else in the country.

"The new coach organized a very simple strategy to get us to win. He did something I found remarkable. He organized the team to minimize each guy's individual weaknesses.

"Yes, weaknesses. He did not let each of us do what we stank at. He did that to minimize our mistakes. If a guy could not dribble, he'd say, 'Fine, you don't dribble—you set up blocks, or you get rebounds. You are good at those things.' If another guy was not a good shooter but was a good play-maker, then we did not throw the guy the ball unless he was really open. We had a bunch of players who would not have made the freshman basketball team anywhere else. We were not the best athletes in the conference."

Nonetheless, the results were amazing. "My junior year we won half our games. My senior year we had the longest winning streak in the nation and had the least points scored against us."

Koch was in much the same position once he found himself literally at the helm of the 1992 America's Cup team. He wasn't the most experienced sailor, but he knew a thing or two about building his team.

"With the America's Cup team, I evaluated the people on talent, teamwork, and attitude." However, to win we also needed technology. That "T^3" leadership concept even found its way into the boat's name: *America*^{3}, pronounced "America cubed."

Koch built the equivalent of a scorecard and evaluated all of his sailors against the criteria, just as you will when you begin using the <u>A</u> Method in your business.

"I rated them on a 1–10 scale in all categories. They had to have a 9 or 10 on attitude and teamwork. I ended up cutting two of the leading sailors in the world because they had a bad attitude. You can't take a superstar and train them to have a good attitude. The same is true with CEOs or key executives."

Next, Koch sourced and selected the most talented sailors

he could find based on his scorecard. He underinvested in this process at first, but quickly saw the value of taking his time.

"One mistake I made was hiring a hot shot out of the America's Cup industry and putting him in charge of the sailing team. He was very charming, very glib. But I had not spent time working with him. Then he tried a hostile takeover and tried to convince the directors to fire me. I said, 'You are out of here. Don't let the doorknob hit you on the way out.'

"I was following the lesson I had learned from my MIT basketball days. I fired the 'best athlete' and took time to hire a replacement who fit his role better. Morale went up. Not everybody was good at everything. They just had to be exceptional at one thing. We hired and organized this way, which is unheard of in the sailing industry."

Vegas gave *America*[3] 100-to-1 odds against winning, and at least two dozen newspapers predicted the Koch-led *America*[3] team would be watching the other boats' wakes.

Imagine, then, the crew's excitement when they found themselves leading the favored Italian entry by just seconds in the final race. Koch described for us the eerie calm that swept over the crew as individual members focused totally on the job at hand. Each one gave everything he had to his individually designed role, and each role was planned to maximize particular skills.

Now imagine how they must have felt when they crossed the finish line.

In first place.

Photo reprinted with permission from Bill Koch.

The Americans beat the heavily favored Italian team by forty-four seconds.

Imagine the excitement of that!

And imagine how excited you will be when the <u>A</u> Method helps you assemble the same kind of top talent and the same type of focused purpose. If Bill Koch can use this method to overcome crazy odds and win the America's Cup with very little background in sailing, you can successfully use this method to improve the performance of your part of your business.

169

Whether you are involved in international sailing competitions, the global marketplace, or the fight to do good for the environment or the planet's neediest, the $\underline{A}$ Method will help you win.

Who, not *what.*

That's the path to your career, financial, and personal success.

And you can do it.

Implementing the $\underline{A}$ Method for Hiring will not only answer that all-important *who* question. It will give you a *who* lens through which to view your entire business. Suddenly you'll find yourself outperforming bigger and more established competitors.

To figure out the scorecard for what matters in a job, just think about what success looks like for the role and how you could measure it through metrics or observation.

To source the talent you need, use the tactics we described from some of the most successful managers in the world. Tap into your networks for referrals and get A Players flowing toward your business. Use recruiters when necessary. Build capabilities within your internal recruiting team.

Select people by going through the rigorous interview process we taught you. Use the skill-will bull's-eye to match A Players to your scorecard with an astounding degree of accuracy.

And sell A Players to take the positions you need them to fill by remembering the five F's of selling to seal the deal.

The $\underline{A}$ Method for Hiring is simple.

The $\underline{A}$ Method works.

The <u>A</u> Method will help you go further.

You have the knowledge to solve your number one problem. You know how to make better *who* decisions.

Today, you just have to decide to act.

Tomorrow, you will enjoy more career success, make more money, and have more time for your relationships that matter most.

We wish you great success as you shift your focus from chasing the *what,* to solving the *who.*

TEACH YOUR MANAGERS HOW TO HIRE
Achieve More Career and Financial Success

KEYNOTES AND WORKSHOPS

Topic: Who: The <u>A</u> Method for Hiring

Return on Investment: 100×1 if your hiring success rate improves just 10 percent.

Features:
- Keynote event with Randy Street or Geoff Smart
- Intensive, day-long workshops with your senior executives
- Train-the-trainer selection, preparation, and coordination

- Books, easy-to-use <u>A</u> Method for Hiring materials, video and audio refreshers
- Total client satisfaction guarantee

Visit www.ghsmart.com to learn more.

BEST CAREER OPPORTUNITY

Would you like to learn about the best job on the planet? If you are an extremely high performer who wants to make a significant positive impact on companies and help leaders be more successful, and you want to enjoy a great lifestyle in addition to creating significant personal wealth, please consider joining ghSMART.

Due to record client satisfaction and rising demand for our services, ghSMART is actively recruiting consultants in North America, Europe, and Asia. If you are interested in learning more about a career at ghSMART, please visit our Web site at www.ghsmart.com.

BIOGRAPHIES OF
CAPTAINS OF INDUSTRY

We thought that you would appreciate learning from some truly exceptional leaders about how they solve their number-one problem. *Exclusively for this book project,* we interviewed more than eighty truly exceptional businesspeople, whom we affectionately refer to as "captains of industry."

We interviewed them in person and on the phone. All of the interviews were conducted personally and originally for this book and in no cases are their ideas reproduced from existing articles or books.

Statistics on the Field Interviews with Captains of Industry

- Billionaires = over 20. This is the largest sample of billionaires ever interviewed for a business book. Some are explicitly identified as billionaires in the biographies below, while others specifically requested to keep the degree of their wealth private.

- CEOs of multibillion-dollar companies = 25.
- CEOs of entrepreneurial companies = 17.
- Private equity investors who live or die based on investing in the right *who* = 23.
- Other = 16, including 1 four-star general and former U.S. presidential candidate, 1 headmaster of a private high school, 1 artist, 3 bestselling authors, 3 leading recruiters, 1 head of HR for a Fortune 500 company, 1 president of a nonprofit, and 1 CFO of a Fortune 500 company.

Please note that in some cases, captains fell into more than one category (e.g., a billionaire who is also CEO of a multibillion-dollar company would count as both).

Captains of Industry

Michael J. Ahearn: CEO, First Solar, Inc. After installing the A Method for Hiring, company went public and grew over ten times in value in one year. The stock was the top performing small- or mid-cap equity of 2007 in the United States.

Gregory Alexander: founder and CEO, Sales Benchmark Index, Inc. The highest-rated sales executive we have ever assessed.

Panos Anastassiadis: chairman, CEO, and president, Cyveillance. Grew the value of his company 1,500 percent over five years.

Jeffrey H. Aronson: co-founder and managing principal, Centerbridge Partners, L.P., the largest first-time private equity fund.

Selim Bassoul: chairman and CEO, Middleby Corporation. Grew value of his company across five years over 3,500 percent while the S&P 500 grew 12 percent.

George W. Buckley: chairman, president, and CEO, 3M.

Charles Butt: billionaire chairman and CEO, H. E. Butt Grocery Company, a $14 billion supermarket company operating in Texas and Mexico.

Carol Campbell: VP human resources, First Solar, Inc.

Dennis C. Carey: partner, Spencer Stuart. CEO super-recruiter.

Michael Cavanagh: CFO, JPMorgan Chase.

Nicholas D. Chabraja: CEO, General Dynamics Corporation, which has been number one in stock performance in the defense and aerospace industry over the last decade.

James Champy: chairman, Perot Systems Consulting Practice; author of *Reengineering the Corporation*.

Wesley K. Clark: retired four-star general, U.S. Army; former U.S. presidential candidate.

Scott Clawson: CEO of GSI; former president of Danaher's most profitable division.

Eric Cohen: managing partner, WHI Capital Partners, a private equity firm.

James Crown: president, Henry Crown & Company; chairman of the board of trustees, University of Chicago; board member of JPMorgan Chase, Sara Lee Corporation, and General Dynamics.

Richard DeVos: billionaire co-founder, Amway, a multibillion-dollar company with 13,000 employees and three million independent business owners globally; owner and chairman of the NBA Orlando Magic.

Barry Diller: billionaire chairman and CEO, IAC; chairman, Expedia, Inc.

Jamie Dimon: chairman and CEO, JPMorgan Chase. Widely regarded as one of the best CEOs alive today.

Gabriel Echavarría: chairman and director, Corona S.A. Organization.

Ed Evans: EVP and chief personnel officer, Allied Waste Industries, a $6 billion waste-hauling company whose stock rose 67 percent over eighteen months (after being flat for five years) after implementing the A Method for Hiring.

Morton Fleischer: founder, Franchise Finance Corporation of America, which was sold to GE Capital in 2001; co-founder and chairman, Spirit Finance Corporation, which was sold to a private equity consortium including Macquarie Bank Limited of Australia and Kaupthing Bank of Iceland. He remains chairman of the board of Spirit Finance companies.

Mark Gallogly: co-founder and managing principal, Centerbridge Partners, L.P., the largest first-time private equity fund.

John T. Gardner: vice chairman, Heidrick & Struggles. Superstar CEO recruiter.

Robert J. Gillette: president and CEO, Honeywell Aerospace, a $12 billion company.

Marshall Goldsmith: executive coach and author whose 2007 book, *What Got You Here Won't Get You There,* was ranked America's number-one bestselling business book by both *The New York Times* and *The Wall Street Journal.*

James A. Gordon: founder and managing partner, the Edgewater Funds.

Alec Gores: billionaire founder and chairman, the Gores Group, a private equity firm. He established the Gores Group after growing and selling his own entrepreneurial companies.

Ken Griffin: billionaire founder, president, and CEO, Citadel Investment Group.

John R. Hall: retired chairman, Ashland Inc., a Fortune 500 Company; served on the board of directors of Bank One, Humana, and USEC.

George Hamilton: president, Institute for Sustainable Communities, a nonprofit that takes a business-minded approach to strengthening communities in the United States and around the world.

J. Tomilson Hill: vice chairman, the Blackstone Group; president and CEO, the Blackstone Marketable Alternative Investments (BAAM) group.

John Howard: CEO, BSMB, a private equity firm.

H. Wayne Huizenga: billionaire chairman, Huizenga Holdings, Inc. The only person to have founded three Fortune 500 companies.

Robert J. Hurst: formerly vice chairman, Goldman Sachs; currently managing director, Crestview Advisors.

E. Neville Isdell: chairman of the board of directors, and former CEO, the Coca-Cola Company.

William R. Johnson: chairman, president, and CEO, H. J. Heinz Corporation.

Paul Tudor Jones: billionaire president and founder, Tudor Investment Corporation.

John W. "Jay" Jordan: chairman and CEO, the Jordan Company, a diversified holding company.

Steven N. Kaplan, Dr.: Neubauer Family Professor of Entrepreneurship and Finance, University of Chicago Graduate School of Business.

Aaron Kennedy: founder and chairman, Noodles & Company. Grew company from zero to 225 stores nationwide.

Steve Kerr: former managing director and chief learning officer, the Goldman Sachs Group, Inc. Known for establishing Crotonville, an executive learning program, for Jack Welch at General Electric.

Tom Kichler: partner, One Equity Partners.

Michael Klein: president, Littlejohn & Co., a private equity firm.

William Ingraham Koch: billionaire founder and president, the Oxbow Group; winner of the 1992 America's Cup sailboat race.

Paul Lattanzio: senior managing director, BGCP, a division of BSMB, a private equity company.

Sir Terry Leahy: CEO, Tesco PLC, the largest retailer in the United Kingdom.

Matt Levin: managing director, Bain Capital, a leading global private investment firm with over $65 billion of assets under management.

Edward M. Liddy: chairman, the Allstate Corporation; serves on the board of directors of the Goldman Sachs Group, Inc., 3M, and the Boeing Company.

Carl Lindner: billionaire chairman and founder, American Financial Group.

Martin Lipton: founder, Wachtell, Lipton, Rosen & Katz, one of the world's leading law firms.

John C. Malone: chairman, Liberty Media Corporation; former CEO, cable giant TCI, the number-one public stock performer in the United States over a two-decade period.

Joe Mansueto: billionaire founder, chairman, and CEO, Morningstar, Inc., a leading global investment research firm.

Roger Marino: billionaire co-founder, EMC Corporation.

Andrew McNally IV: partner, HKW, a private equity firm; former CEO and controlling shareholder, Rand McNally.

Ward S. McNally: founder, president, and CEO, McNally Capital.

Timothy Meyer: VP operations, the Gores Group, a private equity firm.

Adam J. Meyers: chief executive, Halma Health Optics and Photonics Division, Halma PLC, a global health and safety technology company.

Geoffrey E. Molson: vice president, marketing, Molson Coors Brewing Company. Seventh-generation family member of North America's oldest brewery (est. 1786).

Kolia O'Connor: head of school, Sewickley Academy, an independent pre-K through grade twelve school in Western Pennsylvania.

Lee Pillsbury: chairman and CEO, Thayer Lodging Group, a privately held real-estate operating company managing total assets in excess of $2 billion.

Jack Polsky: president and CEO, William Harris Investors, Inc.

Penny Pritzker: billionaire founder, chairman, and CEO, Classic Residence by Hyatt; chairman, TransUnion; president and CEO, Pritzker Realty Group, L.P.

Mike Pyles: head of human capital and development, Citadel Investment Group; formerly HR leader, GE Capital.

Andrea Redmond: consultant and executive recruiter, formerly of Russell Reynolds.

Arthur Rock: billionaire venture capitalist who invested in start-ups Apple, Intel, Teledyne, and many others.

Patrick G. Ryan: billionaire chairman and founder, Aon Corporation, a Fortune 500 insurance brokerage firm with $12 billion in market cap and $9 billion in revenue.

Stacy Schusterman: chairman and CEO, Samson Investment Company, with an annual oil and gas budget of $1.3 billion.

Stephen A. Schwarzman: billionaire chairman, CEO, and cofounder, the Blackstone Group, which manages close to $100 billion in capital.

John Sharpe: chairman of the board, Empire Resorts; former president and COO, Four Seasons.

Brad Smart: president, Topgrading, Inc., and co-creator of Topgrading.

Mark Stone: senior managing director, the Gores Group, a private equity firm; former CEO, Sentient Jet.

Bill Story: owner and president, Ferrari and Maserati of Newport Beach, one of the largest Ferrari and Maserati dealerships in the world.

Spar Street: internationally acclaimed artist, whose artworks uplift and inspire many of the world's most influential individuals and institutions including Ted Turner, Sir Richard Branson, the Sultan of Brunei, numerous CEOs, many best-selling authors, A-list movie stars and musicians, and the United Nations.

Kelvin Thompson: managing partner, Heidrick & Struggles, a global private equity and venture capital practice.

Nathan Thompson: founder and CEO, Spectra Logic Corporation.

John Varley: group chief executive, Barclays.

Erik Vonk: two-time CEO, who grew the value of his last two companies over 700 percent.

Jon Weber: former COO for activist shareholder billionaire Carl Icahn.

Doug Williams: CEO, iHealth Technologies.

John Zillmer: chairman and CEO, Allied Waste Industries, a $6 billion waste-hauling company whose stock rose 67 percent over eighteen months (after being flat for five years) after implementing the A Method for Hiring.

ACKNOWLEDGMENTS

We sincerely appreciate all of the help that wise and generous people gave to us along this journey.

ghSMART is indebted to the hundreds of clients and tens of thousands of workshop participants who have contributed to our thinking over the past thirteen years. Without our clients, there would be no insights, no advice, no stories, and no book.

During the exclusive research work we did for this book, we had the unbelievably exciting opportunity to collect advice and stories from eighty of the most impressive business leaders you could ever meet.

We've listed these "captains of industry" in the preceding pages, and owe a debt of gratitude to every single one of them.

In addition, we are extremely thankful for the work of Dr.

Steve Kaplan and his research team at the Graduate School of Business at the University of Chicago. Steve, with Morten Sorensen and Mark Klebanov, matched the results of 313 CEOs we assessed from 2000 to 2005 to uncover the startling realities that we describe with the terms "Cheetah" and "Lamb." We debated the unconventional findings over espressos in Steve's office, and look forward to continued research with Steve and his team to better understand this phenomenon.

We thank our Harvard research team, Josh Bellin and Ganesh Krishna, for tirelessly searching through the literature on CEO success to find what little has been published about it. We also thank them for compiling the results from our field interviews with our captains of industry.

We'd have been hypocritical if we hadn't used our own method to find our agent and publishing team, and we are so glad we did! We are extremely grateful to our agent, Helen Rees, for guiding us on this journey into the world of publishing. She is an A Player if ever there was one. And she further helped us by introducing us to her son, Lorin Rees, whose guiding hand helped us create an A proposal to share with publishers.

Tim Bartlett, the Random House editor that Helen found for us, has been fantastic to work with. We know not many authors can make that claim. People we called for references told us that Tim was one of the best in the field. They were right. Thank you, Tim, for nurturing a rough manuscript into a book we are proud to share with the world. We thank

University of Chicago/ghSMART research team. From left, Geoff Smart, Mark Klebanov, Morten Sorensen, Steve Kaplan, Randy Street.

Howard Means as well, who gave the book its final polish with Tim's support. And, of course, we are grateful to the entire Random House/Ballantine Books team, whose belief in this project gave it the push that it needed.

We have great appreciation for the influence of Brad Smart, who encouraged Geoff to consider a career in management assessment beginning at the age of twelve. Brad also has been a wonderful thought partner with whom we began developing and refining the concept of Topgrading in 1997.

Marshall Goldsmith gave us some key insights about how to navigate the publishing industry. Paul Lattanzio, John Zillmer, and Ed Evans all read our early drafts and provided candid feedback that helped us smooth out the rough edges.

And many others, too many to list, offered advice and feedback along the way.

Finally, we are thankful to the entire ghSMART team for conducting the SmartAssessments® used in the statistical research, and for crafting the intellectual property on the elusive topic of hiring, which evolved into this book.

ABOUT THE AUTHORS

GEOFF SMART is chairman and and founder of ghSMART, an advisory firm that exists to help leaders amplify their positive impact on the world. He is author of the *New York Times* bestseller *Leadocracy* and co-author of *Power Score*.

geoffsmart.com

RANDY STREET is managing partner of ghSMART and co-author of *Power Score*. He is a leadership advisor to boards and CEOs, and an internationally acclaimed public speaker.

randyhstreet.com